EGOTISM IN
GERMAN PHILOSOPHY

EGOTISM IN
GERMAN PHILOSOPHY

BY
GEORGE SANTAYANA

NEW YORK
CHARLES SCRIBNER'S SONS
1940

NEW PREFACE

AFTER this little book had lain neglected for more than twenty years, an opportune moment seems to the publishers to have arrived for putting it again before the public. Although it passed for a war-book, it was really philosophical, and in the political direction perhaps premature. What is now called ideology was not yet current in British or American politics; and my criterion of criticism belonged to a *philosophia perennis* that nobody wished to listen to in those self-satisfied progressive days. I had wondered if the strain of so terrible a war might not have shaken that optimism and aroused interest in the rationale of idealism, moralism, and human absoluteness in general; but on the whole I was disappointed. Conduct was felt to be bluntly right or wrong apart from all theories or temperaments, and the storm once over, people meant to live on exactly as before. It seemed to many that I was taking an unworthy advantage of public resentment against particular acts of the German Government in order to justify my prejudice against German philosophy. Few people had actually read the German authors to whom I referred or could see the care and even the sympathy with which my brief commentary was composed; and of these few, some of the most competent were perhaps wounded in their own hearts by my criticisms, and found it easier to dismiss than to discuss them. They may have felt only too deeply that I was not attacking something exclusively German but rather the universal prepotency of will and ambition in man, asserting themselves against his finitude. Was I not covertly denying the supremacy of spirit in the universe? It would not be my somewhat playful pen, they were confident, that could propose anything worth considering on such a sacred subject.

I am not sure that my difficulties with German philosophy should be called prejudices, since I have always wished to overcome them, and to understand this philosophy, and every other, sympathetically from the inside. No doubt I have failed at many points, since human faculties are limited and it is impossible altogether to overcome the bias of temperament and tradition. Nor is it morally desirable to do so. The full truth is there in any case, to be viewed and reported from every angle, and not to be added to or subtracted from by incidental apprehension; while this apprehension becomes juster and less deceptive when it admits how partial and poetical it has to be. Now there is an obvious animus pervading these pages, which it was a pleasure for me to vent. I had chafed for years under the pressure of a prim, academic idealism, derived from the German; it professed to be the inescapable philosophy of the day, but I was sure that the dawn of the next day would dissipate it. Moreover, war was raging in a dense fog of war, and although I was legally a neutral throughout the struggle, my sympathies were warmly engaged upon the anti-German side. I was living in England, I was filled with admiration for the simplicity and steadiness of the British temper under trial, and I also felt the contagion of the prevalent sentiment in the United States, where I had spent most of my life. There are phrases in this book that betray these accidental influences and some topical allusions to the events of the hour. I should not now repeat them, but I leave them unaltered, in order that the text may stand absolutely as it was written and that there may be no suspicion of sentiments or prophecies re-edited after the event. I only add, in a Postscript, some later reflections on the nature of egotism and of the moral conflicts that disturb the world.

G. S.

CORTINA D'AMPEZZO,
August 1939.

PREFACE TO THE ORIGINAL EDITION

THIS book is one of the many that the present war has brought forth, but it is the fruit of a long gestation. During more than twenty years, while I taught philosophy at Harvard College, I had continual occasion to read and discuss German metaphysics. From the beginning it wore in my eyes a rather questionable shape. Under its obscure and fluctuating tenets I felt something sinister at work, something at once hollow and aggressive. It seemed a forced method of speculation, producing more confusion than it found, and calculated chiefly to enable practical materialists to call themselves idealists and rationalists to remain theologians. At the same time the fear that its secret might be eluding me, seeing that by blood and tradition I was perhaps handicapped in the matter, spurred me to great and prolonged efforts to understand what confronted me so bewilderingly. I wished to be as clear and just about it as I could—more clear and just, indeed, than it ever was about itself.

For the rest, German philosophy was never my chief interest, and I write frankly as an outsider, with no professorial pretensions; merely using my common

reason in the presence of claims put forth by others
to a logical authority and a spiritual supremacy which
they are far from possessing.

A reader indoctrinated in the German schools is,
therefore, free not to read further. My object is neither
to repeat his familiar arguments in their usual form,
nor to refute them; my object is to describe them intelligibly and to judge them from the point of view of
the layman, and in his interests. For those who wish
to study German philosophy, the original authors are
at hand: all I would give here is the aroma of German
philosophy that has reached my nostrils. If the reader
has smelt something of the kind, so much the better:
we shall then understand each other. The function
of history or of criticism is not passively to reproduce
its subject-matter. One real world, with one stout
corpus of German philosophy, is enough. Reflection
and description are things superadded, things which
ought to be more winged and more selective than what
they play upon. They are echoes of reality in the sphere
of art, sketches which may achieve all the truth appropriate to them without belying their creative limitations: for their essence is to be intellectual symbols,
at once indicative and original.

Egotism — subjectivity in thought and wilfulness
in morals—which is the soul of German philosophy,
is by no means a gratuitous thing. It is a genuine
expression of the pathetic situation in which any animal

finds itself upon earth, and any intelligence in the universe. It is an inevitable and initial circumstance in life. But like every material accident, it is a thing to abstract from and to discount as far as possible. The perversity of the Germans, the childishness and sophistry of their position, lies only in glorifying what is an inevitable impediment, and in marking time on an earthly station from which the spirit of man—at least in spirit—is called to fly.

This glorified and dogged egotism, which a thousand personal and technical evidences had long revealed to me in German philosophy, might now, I should think, be evident to the whole world. Not that the German philosophers are responsible for the war, or for that recrudescence of corporate fanaticism which prepared it from afar. They merely shared and justified prophetically that spirit of uncompromising self-assertion and metaphysical conceit which the German nation is now reducing to action. It is a terrible thing to have a false religion, all the more terrible the deeper its sources are in the human soul. Like many a false religion before it, this which now inspires the Germans has made a double assault upon mankind, one with the secular arm, and another by solemn asseverations and sophistries. This assault, though its incidental methods may be dubious, has been bold and honest enough in principle. It has been like those which all conquerors and all founders of militant religions have made at intervals against liberty or reason. And the issue will doubtless be the same. Liberty may be maimed, but not killed; reason may be bent, but not broken. The dark aggression is to be repelled, if possible, by force of arms; but failing that, it will be nullified in time by the indomitable moral resistance which maturer races, richer in wisdom, can exert successfully against the rude will of the conqueror.

G. S.

1916.

CONTENTS

CHAPTER I

THE GENERAL CHARACTER OF GERMAN PHILOSOPHY

WHAT I propose in these pages to call German philosophy is not identical with philosophy in Germany. The religion of the Germans is foreign to them; and the philosophy associated with religion before the Reformation, and in Catholic circles since, is a system native to the late Roman Empire. Their irreligion is foreign too; the sceptical and the scientific schools that have been conspicuous in other countries have taken root in Germany as well. Thus, if we counted the Catholics and the old-fashioned Protestants on the one hand, and the materialists (who call themselves monists) on the other, we should very likely discover that the majority of intelligent Germans held views which German philosophy proper must entirely despise, and that this philosophy seemed as strange to them as to other people.

For an original and profound philosophy has arisen in Germany, as distinct in genius and method from Greek and Catholic philosophy as this is from the Indian systems. The great characteristic of German philosophy is that it is deliberately subjective and limits itself

B   I

to the articulation of self-consciousness. The whole world appears there, but at a certain remove; it is viewed and accepted merely as an idea framed in consciousness, according to principles fetched from the most personal and subjective parts of the mind, such as duty, will, or the grammar of thought. The direction in which German philosophy is profound is the direction of inwardness. Whatever we may think of its competence in other matters, it probes the self—as unaided intro-spection may—with extraordinary intentness and sincerity. In inventing the transcendental method, the study of subjective projections and perspectives, it has added a new dimension to human speculation.

The foreign religion and the foreign irreligion of Germany are both incompatible with German philosophy. This philosophy cannot accept any dogmas, for its fundamental conviction is that there are no existing things except imagined ones: God as much as matter is exhausted by the thought of Him, and entirely resident in this thought. The notion that knowledge can *discover* anything, or that anything previously existing can be revealed, is discarded altogether: for there is nothing to discover, and even if there were, the mind could not reach it; it could only reach the idea it might call up from its own depths. This idea might be perhaps justified and necessary by virtue of its subjective roots in the will or in duty, but never justified by its supposed external object, an object

SUBJECTIVISM

with which nobody could ever compare it. German philosophy is no more able to believe in God than in matter, though it must talk continually of both.

At the same time this subjectivism is not irreligious. It is mystical, faithful, enthusiastic: it has all the qualities that gave early Protestantism its religious force. It is rebellious to external authority, conscious of inward light and of absolute duties. It is full of faith, if by faith we understand not definite beliefs held on inadequate evidence, but a deep trust in instinct and destiny.

Rather than religious, however, this philosophy is romantic. It accepts passionately the aims suggested to it by sentiment or impulse. It despises prudence and flouts the understanding. In *Faust* and in *Pier Gynt* we have a poetic echo of its fundamental inspiration freed from theological accommodations or academic cant. It is the adventure of a wild, sensitive, boyish mind, that now plays the fairy prince and now the shabby and vicious egoist; a rebel and an enthusiast, yet often a sensualist to boot by way of experiment; a man eager for experience, but blind to its lessons, vague about nature, and blundering about duty, but confident that he can in some way play the magician and bring the world round to serve his will and spiritual necessities.

Happiness and despair are alike impossible with such a temperament. Its empiricism is perennial. It cannot lose faith in the vital impulse it expresses; all its fancy,

3

ingenuity, and daring philosophy are embroideries which it makes upon a dark experience. It cannot take outer facts very seriously; they are but symbols of its own unfathomable impulses. So pensive animals might reason. The just and humble side of German philosophy—if we can lend it virtues to which it is deeply indifferent—is that it accepts the total relativity of the human mind and luxuriates in it, much as we might expect spiders or porpoises to luxuriate in their special sensibility, making no vain effort to peep through the bars of their psychological prison.

This sort of agnosticism in a minor key is conspicuous in the *Critique of Pure Reason*. In a major key it re-appears in Nietzsche, when he proclaims a preference for illusion over truth. More mystically expressed it pervades the intervening thinkers. The more profound they are, the more content and even delighted they are to consider nothing but their own creations. Their theory of knowledge proclaims that knowledge is im-possible. You know only your so-called knowledge, which itself knows nothing; and you are limited to the autobiography of your illusions.

The Germans express this limitation of their philo-sophy by calling it idealism. In several senses it fully deserves this name. It is idealistic psychologically in that it regards mental life as groundless and all-inclusive, and denies that a material world exists, except as an idea necessarily bred in the mind. It is

4

idealistic, too, in that it puts behind experience a background of concepts, and not of matter; a ghostly framework of laws, categories, moral or logical principles to be the stiffening and skeleton of sensible experience, and to lend it some substance and meaning. It is idealistic in morals also, in that it approves of pursuing the direct objects of will, without looking over one's shoulder or reckoning the consequences. These direct objects are ideals, whereas happiness, or any satisfaction based on renunciation and compromise, seems to these spirited philosophers the aim of a degraded, calculating mind. The word idealism, used in this sense, should not mislead us; it indicates sympathy with life and its passions, particularly the learned and political ones; it does not indicate any distaste for material goods or material agencies. The German moral imagination is in its first or dogmatic stage, not in the second or critical one. It is in love with life rather than with wisdom.

There is accordingly one sense of the term idealism —the original one—in which this philosophy knows nothing of it, the Platonic and poetic sense in which the ideal is something *better* than the fact. The Platonic idealist is the man by nature so wedded to perfection that he sees in everything not the reality but the faultless ideal which the reality misses and suggests. Hegel, indeed, drew an outline portrait of things, according to what he thought their ideal essence; but it was uglier and more dreary than the things themselves. Platonic idealism requires a gift of impassioned contemplation, an incandescent fancy that leaps from the things of sense to the goals of beauty and desire. It spurns the earth and believes in heaven, a form of religion most odious to the Germans. They think this sort of idealism not only visionary but somewhat impious; for their own religion takes the form of piety and affection towards everything homely, imperfect, unstable, and progressive. They yearn to pursue the unattainable and encounter the unforeseen. This romantic craving hangs together with their taste for the picturesque and emphatic in the plastic arts, and for the up-welling evanescent emotions of music. Yet their idealism is a religion of the actual. It rejects nothing in the daily experience of life, and looks to nothing essentially different beyond. It looks only for more of the same thing, believing in perpetual growth, which is an ambiguous notion. Under the fashionable name of progress what these idealists sincerely cherish is the vital joy of transition; and usually the joy of this transition lies much more in shedding their present state than in attaining a better one. For they suffer and wrestle continually, and by a curious and deeply animal instinct, they hug and sanctify this endless struggle all the more when it rends and bewilders them, bravely declaring it to be absolute, infinite, and divine.

Such in brief is German philosophy, at least, such it might be said to be if any clear account of it did not necessarily falsify it; but one of its chief characteristics, without which it would melt away, is ambiguity. You cannot maintain that the natural world is the product of the human mind without changing the meaning of the word mind and of the word human. You cannot deny that there is a substance without turning into a substance whatever you substitute for it. You cannot identify yourself with God without at once asserting and denying the existence of God and of yourself. When you speak of such a thing as the consciousness of society you must never decide whether you mean the consciousness individuals have of society or a fabled consciousness which society is to have of itself: the first meaning would spoil your eloquence, and the second would betray your mythology.

What is involved in all these equivocations is not merely a change of vocabulary, that shifting use of language which time brings with it. No, the persistence of the old meanings alone gives point to the assertions that change them and identify them with their opposites. Everywhere, therefore, in these speculations, you must remain in suspense as to what precisely you are talking about. A vague, muffled, dubious thought must carry you along as on a current. Your scepticism must not derange your common sense; your conduct must not express your radical opinions; a certain afflatus must bear you nobly onward through a perpetual incoherence. You must always be thinking not of what you are thinking of but of yourself or of 'something higher.' Otherwise you cannot live this philosophy or understand it from within.

The mere existence of this system, as of any other, proves that a provocation to frame it is sometimes found in experience or language or the puzzles of reflection. Not that there need be any solidity in it on that account. German philosophy is a sort of religion, and like other religions it may be capable of assimilating a great amount of wisdom, while its first foundation is folly. This first folly itself will not lack plausible grounds; there is provocation enough in a single visit to a madhouse for the assertion that the mind can know nothing but the ideas it creates; nevertheless the assertion is false, and such facile scepticism loses sight of the essence of knowledge. The most disparate minds, since they do not regard themselves, may easily regard the same object. Only the maniac stares at his own ideas; he confuses himself in his perceptions; he projects them into the wrong places, and takes surrounding objects to be different from what they are. But perceptions originally have external objects; they express a bodily reaction, or some inward preparation for such a reaction. They are reports. The porpoise and the spider are not shut up in their self-consciousness; however foreign to us may be the language of their senses, they know the sea and air that we know, and have to meet the same changes and accidents there which we meet—and they even have to meet us, sometimes, to their sorrow. Their knowledge does not end in acquaintance with that sensuous language of theirs, whatever it may be, but flies with the import of that language and salutes the forces which confront them in action, and which also confront us. In focusing these forces through the lenses and veils of sense knowledge arises; and to arrest our attention on those veils and lenses and say they are all we know, belies the facts of the case and is hardly honest. If we could really do that, we should be retracting the first act of intelligence and becoming artificial idiots. Yet this sophistication is the first principle of German philosophy (borrowed, indeed, from non-Germans), and is the thesis supposed to be proved in Kant's *Critique of Pure Reason*.

CHAPTER II

THE PROTESTANT HERITAGE

THE German people, according to Fichte and Hegel, are called by the plan of Providence to occupy the supreme place in the history of the universe.

A little consideration of this belief will perhaps lead us more surely to the heart of German philosophy than would the usual laborious approach to it through what is called the theory of knowledge. This theory of knowledge is a tangle of equivocations; but even if it were correct it would be something technical, and the technical side of a great philosophy, interesting as it may be in itself, hardly ever determines its essential views. These essential views are derived rather from instincts or traditions which the technique of the system is designed to defend; or, at least, they decide how that technique shall be applied and interpreted.

The moment we hear Fichte and Hegel mentioning a providential plan of the world, we gather that in their view the history of things is not infinite and endlessly various, but has a closed plot like a drama in which one nation (the very one to which these philosophers belong) has the central place and the chief role: and we perceive at once that theirs is a revealed philosophy. It is the heir of Judaism. It could never have been formed by free observation of life and nature, like the philosophy of Greece or of the Renaissance. It is Protestant theology rationalized. The element of religious faith, in the Protestant sense of the word faith, is essential to it. About the witness of tradition, even about the witness of the senses, it may be as sceptical as it likes. It may reduce nature and God to figments of the mind; but throughout its criticism of all matters of fact it will remain deeply persuaded that the questioning and striving spirit within is indefeasible and divine. It will never reduce all things, including the mind, to loose and intractable appearances, as might a free idealism. It will employ its scepticism to turn all things into ideas, in order to chain them the more tightly to the moral interests of the thinker. These moral interests, human and pathetic as they may seem to the outsider, it will exalt immeasurably, pronouncing them to be groundless and immutable; and it will never tolerate the suspicion that all things might not minister to them.

From the same tenet of Fichte and Hegel we may also learn that in the plan of the world, as this revealed philosophy conceives it, the principal figures are not individuals, like the Creator, the Redeemer, and one's own soul, but nations and institutions. It is of the essence of Protestantism and of German philosophy that religion should gradually drop its supernatural personages and comforting private hopes and be absorbed in the duty of living manfully and conscientiously the conventional life of this world. Not the whole life of the world, however, since gay religions and many other gay things are excluded, or admitted only as childish toys. Positive religion, in fact, disappears, as well as the frivolous sort of worldliness, and there remains only a consecrated worldliness that is deliberate and imposed as a duty. Just as in pantheism God is naturalized into a cosmic force, so in German philosophy the Biblical piety of the earlier Protestants is secularized into social and patriotic zeal.

German philosophy has inherited from Protestantism its earnestness and pious intention; also a tendency to retain, for whatever changed views it may put forward, the names of former beliefs. God, freedom, and immortality, for instance, may eventually be transformed into their opposites, since the oracle of faith is internal; but their names may be kept, together with a feeling that what will now bear those names is much more satisfying than what they originally stood for. If it should seem that God came nearest to us, and dwelt within us, in the form of vital energy, if freedom should turn out really to mean personality, if immortality, in the end, should prove identical with the endlessness of human progress, and if these new thoughts should satisfy and encourage us as the evanescent ideas of God, freedom, and immortality satisfied and encouraged our fathers, why should we not use these consecrated names for our new conceptions, and thus indicate the continuity of religion amid the flux of science? This expedient is not always hypocritical. It was quite candid in men like Spinoza and Emerson, whose attachment to positive religion had insensibly given way to a half - mystical, half - intellectual satisfaction with the natural world, as their eloquent imagination conceived it. But whether candid or disingenuous, this habit has the advantage of oiling the wheels of progress with a sacred unction. In facilitating change it blurs the consciousness of change, and leads people to associate with their new opinions sentiments which are logically incompatible with them. The attachment of many tender-minded people to German philosophy is due to this circumstance, for German philosophy is not tender.

The beauty and the torment of Protestantism is that it opens the door so wide to what lies beyond it. This progressive quality it has fully transmitted to all the systems of German philosophy. Not that each of them, like the earlier Protestant sects, does not think itself true and final; but in spite of itself it suggests some next thing. We must expect, therefore, that the more conservative elements in each system should provoke protests in the next generation; and it is hard to say whether such inconstancy is a weakness, or is simply loyalty to the principle of progress. Kant was a puritan;

he revered the rule of right as something immutable and holy, perhaps never obeyed in the world. Fichte was somewhat freer in his Calvinism; the rule of right was the moving power in all life and nature, though it might have been betrayed by a doomed and self-seeking generation. Hegel was a very free and superior Lutheran; he saw that the divine will was necessarily and continuously realized in this world, though we might not recognize the fact in our petty moral judgments. Schopenhauer, speaking again for this human judgment, revolted against that cruel optimism, and was an indignant atheist; and finally, in Nietzsche, this atheism became exultant; he thought it the part of a man to abet the movement of things, however calamitous, in order to appropriate its wild force and be for a moment the very crest of its wave.

Protestantism was not a reformation by accident, because it happened to find the Church corrupt; it is a reformation essentially, in that every individual must reinterpret the Bible and the practices of the Church in his own spirit. If he accepted them without renewing them in the light of his personal religious experience, he would never have what Protestantism thinks living religion. German philosophy has inherited this characteristic; it is not a cumulative science that can be transmitted ready made. It is essentially a reform, a revision of traditional knowledge, which each neophyte must make for himself, under pain of rendering only lip-service to transcendental truth, and remaining at heart unregenerate. His chief business is to be converted; he must refute for himself the natural views with which he and all other men have begun life. And still these views—like the temptations of Satan—inevitably form themselves afresh in each generation, and even in the philosopher, between one spell of introspective thought and another, so that he always has to recapitulate his saving arguments from the beginning. Each new idealist in each of his books, often in every lecture and every chapter, must run back to refute again the same homely opponents—materialism, naturalism, dualism, or whatever he may call them. Dead as each day he declares these foes to be, he has to fight them again in his own soul on the morrow. Hence his continual preoccupation lest he fall away, or lest the world should forget him. To preserve his freedom and his idealism he must daily conquer them anew. This philosophy is secondary, critical, sophistical; it has a perennial quarrel with inevitable opinions.

Protestantism, in spite of its personal status, wished to revert to primitive Christianity. In this desire it was guided partly by a conventional faith in the Scriptures, and partly by a deep sympathy with experimental religion. German religion and philosophy are homesick: they wish to be quite primitive once more. And they actually remain primitive in spirit, spontaneous

15

and tentative, even in the midst of the most cumbrous erudition, as a composition of Dürer's, where flesh, fish, and fowl crowd every corner, still remains primitive, puzzled, and oppressed. Such a naïve but overloaded mind is lost in admiration of its own depth and richness; yet, in fact, it is rather helpless and immature; it has not learned to select what suffices, or to be satisfied with what is best.

Faith for the Germans must be a primitive and groundless assurance, not knowledge credibly transmitted by others whose experience may have been greater than our own. Even philosophy is not conceived as a reasonable adjustment to what may have been discovered to be the constitution of the world; it is in the first instance a criticism, to dissolve that reputed knowledge, and then, when primitive innocence is happily restored, it is a wager or demand made beyond all evidence, and in contempt of all evidence, in obedience to an innate impulse. Of course, it is usual, as a concession to the weaker brethren, to assume that experience, in the end, will seem to satisfy these demands, and that we shall win our bets and our wars; but the point of principle, borrowed by German philosophy from Protestantism, is that the authority of faith is intrinsic and absolute, while any external corroboration of it is problematical and not essential to the rightness of the assumptions that faith makes. In this we have a fundamental characteristic of the school. Carried (as it seldom is) to its logical conclusion, it leads to the ultra-romantic and ultra-idealistic doctrine that the very notion of truth or fact is a fiction of the will, invented to satisfy our desire for some fixed point of reference in thought. In this doctrine we may see the culmination of the Protestant rebellion against mediation in religion, against external authority, and against dogma.

The Protestant precept to search the Scriptures, and the sense that every man must settle the highest questions for himself, have contributed to the zeal with which science and scholarship have been pursued in Germany. In no other country has so large, so industrious, and (amid its rude polemics) so co-operative a set of professors devoted itself to all sorts of learning. But as the original motive was to save one's soul, an apologetic and scholastic manner has often survived: the issue is prejudged and egotism has appeared even in science. For favourable as Protestantism is to investigation and learning, it is almost incompatible with clearness of thought and fundamental freedom of attitude. If the controlling purpose is not political or religious, it is at least 'philosophical,' that is to say, arbitrary.

We must remember that the greater part of the 'facts' on which theories are based are reported or inferred facts—*all* in the historical sciences, since the documents and sources must first be pronounced

c   17

genuine or spurious by the philosophical critic. Here presumptions and private methods of inference determine what shall be admitted for a fact, to say nothing of the interpretation to be given to it. Hence a piece of Biblical or Homeric criticism, a history of Rome or of Germany, often becomes a little system of egotistical philosophy, posited and defended with all the parental zeal and all the increasing conviction with which a prophet defends his supernatural inspirations.

The distinction between Mary and Martha is not a German distinction: in Germany the rapt idealist is busy about many things, so that his action is apt to be heady and his contemplation perturbed. Only the principle is expected to be spiritual, the illustrations must all be material and mundane. There is no paradox in German idealism turning to material science, commerce, and war for a fresh field of operation. No degeneracy is implied in such an extension of its vocation, especially when the other ideals of the State—pure learning, art, social organization—are pursued at the same time with an equal ardour. The test of a genuine German idealist is that he should forget and sink his private happiness in whatever service the State may set him to do.

In view of this political fidelity the changing opinions of men are all indifferent to true religion. It is not a question of *correctness* in opinion or conduct, since for the idealist there can be no external standard of truth, existence, or excellence on which such correctness could depend. Ideas are so much real experience and have no further subject - matter. Thought is simply more or less rich, elaborate, or vehement, like a musical composition, and more or less consistent with itself. It is all a question of depth and fullness of experience, obtained by hacking one's way through this visionary and bewitched existence, the secret purpose of which is to serve the self in its development. In this philosophy imagination that is sustained is called knowledge, illusion that is coherent is called truth, and will that is systematic is called virtue.

Evidently the only sanction or vindication that such a belief will look for is the determination to reassert it. Religion is here its own heaven, and faith the only proof of its own truth. What is harmonized in the end is not the experience through which people have actually passed, but only the echoes of that experience chiming in the mystic ear. Memory too can play the egotist. Subjectivism can rule even within the subject and can make him substitute his idea of himself, in his most self-satisfied moment, for the poor desultory self that he has actually been.

The German philosophers have carried on Protestantism beyond itself. They have separated the two ingredients mingled in traditional religions. One of these ingredients—the vital faith or self-trust of the

animal will — they have retained. The other — the
lessons of experience—they have rejected. To which
element the name of religion should still be given, if it
is given to either, is a matter of indifference. The
important thing is that, call it religion or irreligion, we
should know what we are clinging to.

CHAPTER III

TRANSCENDENTALISM

FICHTE called Locke the worst of philosophers, but it was ungrateful of him, seeing that his own philosophy was founded on one of Locke's errors. It was Locke who first thought of looking into his own breast to find there the genuine properties of gold and of an apple; and it is clear that nothing but lack of consecutiveness and courage kept him from finding the whole universe in the same generous receptacle. This method of looking for reality in one's own breast, when practised with due consecutiveness and courage by the German became the transcendental method; but it must admitted that the German breast was no longer that anatomical region which Locke had intended to probe, but a purely metaphysical point of departure, a migratory ego that could be here, there, and everywhere at once, being present at any point from which thought or volition might be taken to radiate. It was no longer so easy to entrap as the soul of Locke, which he asserted travelled with him in his coach from London to Oxford.

But the practice of looking for all things within one's

own breast, in the subtler sense of searching for them in one's memory and experience, begat in time the whole romantic and subjective school of philosophy.

Leibniz, the first of German philosophers, although an enemy of Locke's sensualism and of his slackness in logic, was even more explicit in assigning a mental seat to all sensible objects. The soul, he said, had no windows and, he might have added, no doors; no light could come to it from without; and it could not exert any transitive force or make any difference beyond its own insulated chamber. It was a *camera obscura*, with a universe painted on its impenetrable walls. The changes which went on in it were like those in a dream, due to the charge of pent-up energies and fecundities within it; for the Creator had wound it up at the creation like a clock, destined to go for ever, striking infinite hours, with ever richer chimes.

Here, in miniature, with a clearness and beauty never afterwards equalled, we have the nature and movement of the transcendental self set forth before us: a closed circle of experience, admitting of no relations with anything beyond, but infinite in its own potential developments, and guided by an inner force, according to an innate unconscious plan. All duties, all principles of interpretation, all data, all visioned objects, operated within this single life, diversifying its field of view, and testifying to its secret endowment.

Nevertheless, the later idealists, ungrateful to Locke

for their first principle, were ungrateful also to Leibniz for their ultimate conception, anticipated by him in all its completeness. There were reasons, of course, for this ingratitude. Leibniz, like the transcendentalists, had supposed that the objects of sense, as experience reveals them, were begotten out of the latent nature of the soul; but he had also conceived that there were many souls, as many as atoms in the physical world, and that the images arising in each were signs of the presence and actual condition of its companions. Thus perception, while yielding directly only an idea, as in a dream, was indirectly symbolic of an outer reality, like a dream significant and capable of interpretation. And being an undaunted rationalist, Leibniz assumed that the soothsayer capable of reading this dream was reason, and that whatever reason conceived to be right and necessary actually must be true in the great outer world.

It was at this point that Kant deviated into his radical subjectification of knowledge. His mind had been more open than that of Leibniz to the influences of English psychology, it had stewed longer in its own juice, and he could not help asking how, if the senses could reveal only ideas of sense, reason was ever able to reveal anything but ideas of reason. Those inferences about the vast world outside, which Leibniz had allowed his spirits to make in their solitary confinement, were reduced by the more scrupulous Kant to scribblings upon their prison walls. These scribblings he officially termed the ideas of pure—that is, of unsupported—reason; but in his private capacity he gently continued to agree with Leibniz and to believe them true.

There was no anomaly, according to Kant, in this situation. An idea might by chance be the image of a reality, but we could never know that it was. For the proof would have to be supplied by a further idea, and would terminate in that. The hypothesis and the corroboration would alike be mental, since experience was of ideas and could envisage nothing but the vicissitudes of the mind.

If you had asked Leibniz what determined the order in which perceptions came into any mind, he would doubtless have answered that the Creator did so, or (translating that symbol into its analytic equivalent in his system) that what did so was the innate destiny or predisposition of that mind to develop in harmony with the best possible universe. Here is a very remarkable unconscious principle of evolution seated in the spirit and presiding over all its experience. This is precisely what is meant by a transcendental principle.

This principle, unconscious as it is, sometimes betrays its mighty workings to consciousness. Besides the incidental multitude of ideas which it breeds, it makes itself felt in subterranean strains and rumblings, in the sense of movement and of longing. This darker but deeper manifestation of the transcendental clockwork Leibniz called appetition, and under the name of Will it has played a great part in later German systems. To call it Will is, of course, to speak improperly and mythologically, for actual willing requires an idea of what is willed. When we say a man doesn't know what he wants, we mean that he can will nothing, for lack of a clear idea of his interests and situation, although he doubtless wants or lacks many specific things, the absence of which is rendering him unhappy and restless. These instinctive appetitions for objects of which the mind is ignorant may, by a figure of speech, be called unconscious Will; a phrase which would be a contradiction in terms if this word Will (which I write with a capital letter) were not used metaphorically. From this metaphor, when its boldness seems to be dulled by use, we may pass insensibly to giving the name of Will to that whole transcendental potency of the soul which, like the mainspring of a watch, lay coiled up tightly within it from the beginning of time. A man's transcendental Will can then be called the source of everything that ever happens to him—his birth, his character, his whole life, and his death—all that he most detests and most emphatically does not will, like his nightmares, being an expression of the original pregnancy of his spirit, and of its transcendental principle of development.

There is but one thing to add touching a point often

left by these philosophers in the most hopeless obscurity. In Leibniz the number of spirits was infinite: in the later systems they are reduced to one. This difference seems greater than it is, for when such terms as Spirit or Will are used metaphorically, standing for unconscious laws of continuity or development, and when the Will or Spirit present in me now may be said to have presided over the destinies of my soul infinite ages before I was born, there seems to be no good reason why the same Spirit or Will should not preside over all the inhabitants of the universe at all times, be they gods or humming-birds. Such a Spirit or Will resembles the notion of Providence, or the law of evolution, or the pre-estab-lished harmony of Leibniz far more than it resembles a mind. Those philosophers, intent on proving that the Spirit can only be one, might have proceeded, therefore, by urging that a Spirit was at best a formal and abstract law, covering such disparate facts, that all flesh and fowl, all demons and angels, might just as well be animated by a single Spirit. As it takes all sorts of things to make a world, it might take all sorts of things to express a Spirit.

This cool and consciously verbal way of making all one, however, is not the way of the Germans. No doubt in practice the unity of the Spirit or Will in their systems amounts to nothing more, yet their intention and illusion is rather that whenever two things can be called manifestations of one Spirit in the loosest and most metaphorical sense of this word they are thereby proved to be data in one Spirit in the most intimate and psychological sense of the same. So that what really happens to transcendentalists is not that they unite all the transcendental units of Leibniz into one even looser transcendental unit, but that they limit the universe to what in Leibniz was one of an infinite number of parallel careers. Nay, they limit even that one career to the experience present at one point, that of the most intense and comprehensive self-consciousness.

The unity they desire and believe in is accordingly an actual and intense unity. All its elements are to be viewed at once, bound and merged together by the simultaneous intuition of all their relations, and this in a single, unchanging, eternal moment of thought, or rather of unutterable feeling. The union is, therefore, real, psychic, mystical, and so close that everything that was to be united there, by a curious irony, remains outside.

What can lead serious thinkers, we may ask, into such pitfalls and shams? In this case, a powerful and not unworthy motive. All transcendentalism takes the point of view of what it calls knowledge; whenever it mentions anything—matter, God, oneself—it means not that thing but the idea of it. By knowledge it understands the image or belief, the fact of cognition. Whatever is thought of exists, or can exist, in this philosophy, only for thought; yet this thought is called not illusion but knowledge, because knowledge is what the thought feels that it is.

Evidently on this principle none of Leibniz's spirits could know any other, nor could any phase of the same spirit know any other phase. The unbridgeable chasm of want of experience would cut off knowledge from everything but its ' content,' the ideas it has of its objects. Those fabled external objects would be brought back into my ideas, and identified with them; my ideas in turn would be drawn in and identified with the fact that I entertain them, and this fact itself would condense into the more intimate and present fact that intensely, vaguely, deeply I feel that I am, or am tending to be, something or other. My Will or Spirit, the rumble of my unconscious appetitions, thus absorbs my ideas, my ideas absorb their objects, and these objects absorb the world, past, present, and future. Earth and heaven, God and my fellow-men are mere expressions of my Will, and if they were anything more, I could not now be alive to their presence. My Will is absolute. With that conclusion transcendentalism is complete.

Is such transcendentalism impossibly sceptical? Is it absurdly arrogant? Is it wonderfully true?

In so complex a world as this, there is room for a great number of cross-vistas: when all has been surveyed from one point of view and in one set of terms, nothing excludes the same reality from being surveyed from a different centre and expressed in a different notation.

To represent a man, sculpture is apparently exhaustive; yet it does not exclude painting, or the utterly disparate description of the man in words; surveys in which there need be no contradiction in the deliverance, though there is the widest diversity and even incommensurability in the methods. Each sort of net drawn through the same sea catches a different sort of fish; and the fishermen may quarrel about what the sea contained, if each regards his draught as exhaustive. Yet the sea contained all their catches, and also the residue, perhaps infinite, that escaped them all.

Now one net which every intelligent being casts over things is that of his own apprehension, experience, and interests. He may not reflect often on his personal principle of selection and arrangement; he may be so interested in the movements he sees through his glass as never to notice the curious circular frame, perhaps prismatic, which his glass imposes on the landscape. Yet among all the properties of things, the adventitious properties imputed to them in apprehension are worth noting too; indeed, it chastens and transforms our whole life if we have once noted them and taken them to heart. Not that this circumstance implies for a moment what the dizziness of idealists has inferred, that things exist only as perceived or when we perceive them. What follows is rather that, besides the things and in the most interesting contrast to their movement, there is the movement of our minds in observing them. If, for instance, I happen not to know the name of my great-grandfather, and am vexed at my ignorance, I may search the parish records and discover it, together with many circumstances of his life. This does not prove that my interest in genealogy created my great-grandfather, as a consistent egotist would assert; but it does show how my interest was a nucleus for my discoveries and for the terms, such as great-grandfather, in which I express them—for it was no intrinsic property of that worthy man that he was to become my great-grandfather after his death, or that I was to discover him.

This vortex which things, as apprehension catches them, seem to form round each whirling spectator, is the fascinating theme of lyric poetry, of psychological novels, and of German philosophy. Dominated as this philosophy is by the transcendental method, it regards views, and the history and logic of views, as more primitive and important than the objects which these views have in common. The genial Professor Paulsen of Berlin (whose pupil I once had the advantage of being) had a phrase that continually recurred in his lectures, *Man kann sagen*, as much as to say, things will yield the following picture, if one cares to draw it. And he once wrote an article in honour of Kant very pertinently entitled *Was uns Kant sein kann*; because no veritable disciple of Kant accepts what Kant taught as he taught it, but each rises from the study of the master having irresistibly formed one or more systems of his own. To take what views we will of things, if things will barely suffer us to take them, and then to declare that the things are mere terms in the views we take of them—that is transcendentalism.

CHAPTER IV

HINTS OF EGOTISM IN GOETHE

ALL transcendentalists are preoccupied with the self, but not all are egotists. Some regard as a sad disability this limitation of their knowledge to what they have created; they are humble, and almost ashamed to be human, and to possess a mind that must cut them off hopelessly from all reality. On the other hand there are many instinctive egotists who are not transcendentalists, either because their attention has not been called to this system, or because they discredit all speculation, or because they see clearly that the senses and the intellect, far from cutting us off from the real things that surround us, have the function of adjusting our action to them and informing our mind about them. Such an instinctive egotist does not allege that he creates the world by willing and thinking it, yet he is more interested in his own sensations, fancies, and preferences than in the other things in the world. The attention he bestows on things seems to him to bathe in light their truly interesting side. What he chiefly considers is his own experience—what he cared for first, what second, what he thinks to-day, what he will probably think to-

morrow, what friends he has had, and how they have
lost their charm, what religions he has believed in, and
in general what contributions the universe has made to
him and he to the universe. His interest in personality
need not be confined to his own; he may have a dramatic
imagination, and may assign their appropriate personality to all other people; every situation he hears of or
invents may prompt him to conceive the thrilling
passions and pungent thoughts of some *alter ego*, in
whom latent sides of his own nature may be richly expressed. And impersonal things, too, may fascinate
him, when he feels that they stir his genius fruitfully;
and he will be the more ready to scatter his favours
broadcast in that what concerns him is not any particular
truth or person (things which might prove jealous and
exclusive), but rather the exercise of his own powers of
universal sympathy.

Something of this sort seems to appear in Goethe;
and although his contact with philosophical egotism
was but slight, and some of his wise maxims are incompatible with it, yet his romanticism, his feeling
for development in everything, his private life, the
nebulous character of his religion, and some of his most
important works, like *Faust* and *Wilhelm Meister*, are
all so full of the spirit of German philosophy, that it
would be a pity not to draw some illustration for our
subject from so pleasant a source.

There are hints of egotism in Goethe, but in Goethe

there are hints of everything, and it would be easy to gather an imposing mass of evidence to the effect that he was not like the transcendentalists, but far superior to them. For one thing he was many - sided, not encyclopaedic; he went out to greet the variety of things, he did not pack it together. He did not even arrange the phases of his experience (as he did those of Faust) in an order supposed to be a progress, although, as the commentators on *Faust* inform us, not a progress in mere goodness. Hegel might have *understood* all these moral attitudes, and described them in a way not meant to appear satirical; but he would have criticized and demolished them, and declared them obsolete—all but the one at which he happened to stop. Goethe *loved* them all; he hated to outgrow them, and if involuntarily he did so, at least he still honoured the feelings that he had lost. He kept his old age genial and green by that perennial love. In order to hold his head above water and be at peace in his own heart, he did not need to be a Christian, a pagan, or an epicurean; yet he lent himself unreservedly, in imagination, to Christianity, paganism, and sensuality — three things your transcendental egotist can never stomach: each in its way would impugn his self-sufficiency.

Nevertheless the sympathies of Goethe were only romantic or aesthetic; they were based on finding in others an interesting variation from himself, an exotic possibility, rather than an identity with himself in thought or in fate. Christianity was an atmosphere necessary to certain figures, that of Gretchen, for instance, who would have been frankly vulgar without it; paganism was a learned masque, in which one could be at once distinguished and emancipated; and sensuality was a sentimental and scientific licence in which the free mind might indulge in due season. The sympathy Goethe felt with things was that of a lordly observer, a traveller, a connoisseur, a philanderer; it was egotistical sympathy.

Nothing, for instance, was more romantic in Goethe than his classicism. His *Iphigenie* and his *Helena* and his whole view of antiquity were full of the pathos of distance. That pompous sweetness, that intense moderation, that moral somnambulism were too intentional; and Goethe felt it himself. In *Faust*, after Helen has evaporated, he makes the hero revisit his native mountains and revert to the thought of Gretchen. It is a wise home-coming, because that craze for classicism which Helen symbolized alienated the mind from real life and led only to hopeless imitations and lackadaisical poses. Gretchen's garden, even the *Walpurgisnacht*, was in truth more classical. This is only another way of saying that in the attempt to be Greek the truly classical was missed even by Goethe, since the truly classical is not foreign to anybody. It is precisely that part of tradition and art which does not alienate us from our own life or from nature, but reveals them in all their depth and nakedness, freed from the fashions and hypocrisies of time and place. The effort to reproduce the peculiarities of antiquity is a proof that we are not its natural heirs, that we do not continue antiquity instinctively. People can mimic only what they have not absorbed. They reconstruct and turn into an archaeological masquerade only what strikes them as outlandish. The genuine inheritors of a religion or an art never dream of reviving it; its antique accidents do not interest them, and its eternal substance they possess by nature.

The Germans are not in this position in regard to the ancients. Whether sympathetic like Goethe, or disparaging like Burckhardt, or both at once, like Hegel, they have seen in antiquity its local colour, its mannerisms, its documents, and above all its contrasts with the present. It was not so while the traditions of antiquity were still living and authoritative. But the moderns, and especially the Germans, have not a humble mind. They do not go to school with the Greeks unfeignedly, as if Greek wisdom might possibly be true wisdom, a pure expression of experience and reason, valid essentially for us. They prefer to take that wisdom for a phase of sentiment, of course outgrown, but still enabling them to reconstruct learnedly the image of a fascinating past. This is what they call giving vitality to classical studies, turning them into *Kulturgeschichte*. This is a vitality lent by the living to the dead, not one drawn by the young and immature from a perennial fountain. In truth classical studies were vital only so long as they were still authoritative morally and set the standard for letters and life. They became otiose and pedantic when they began to serve merely to recover a dead past in its trivial detail, and to make us grow sentimental over its remoteness, its beauty, and its ruins.

How much freer and surer was Goethe's hand when it touched the cord of romanticism! How perfectly he knew the heart of the romantic egotist! The romantic egotist sets no particular limits to the range of his interests and sympathies; his programme, indeed, is to absorb the whole world. He is no wounded and disappointed creature, like Byron, that takes to sulking and naughtiness because things taste bitter in his mouth. He finds good and evil equally digestible. The personal egotism of Byron or of Musset after all was humble; it knew how weak it was in the universe. But absolute egotism in Goethe, as in Emerson, summoned all nature to minister to the self: all nature, if not actually compelled to this service by a human creative fiat, could at least be won over to it by the engaging heroism of her favourite child. In his warm pantheistic way Goethe felt the swarming universal life about him; he had no thought of dragooning it all, as sectarians and nationalists would, into vindicating some particular creed or nation. Yet that fertile and impartial universe left each life free and in uncensored competition with every other life. Each creature might feed blamelessly on all the others and become, if it could, the focus and epitome of the world. The development of self was the only duty, if only the self was developed widely and securely enough, with insight, calmness, and godlike irresponsibility.

Goethe exhibited this principle in practice more plainly, perhaps, than in theory. His family, his friends, his feelings were so many stepping-stones in his moral career; he expanded as he left them behind. His love-affairs were means to the fuller realization of himself. Not that his love-affairs were sensual or his infidelities callous; far from it. They often stirred him deeply and unsealed the springs of poetry in his heart; that was precisely their function. Every tender passion opened before him a primrose path into which his inexorable genius led him to wander. If in passing he must tread down some flower, that was a great sorrow to him; but perhaps that very sorrow and his inevitable remorse were the most needful and precious elements in the experience. Every pathetic sweetheart in turn was a sort of Belgium to him; he violated her neutrality with a sigh; his heart bled for her innocent sufferings, and he never said afterwards in self-defence, like the German Chancellor, that she was no better than she should be. But he must press on. His beckoning destiny, the claims of his spiritual growth, compelled him to sacrifice her and to sacrifice his own lacerated feelings on the altar of duty to his infinite self. Indeed, so truly supreme was this vocation that universal nature too, he thought, was bound to do herself some violence in his behalf and to grant him an immortal life, that so noble a process of self-expansion might go on for ever.

Goethe's perfect insight into the ways of romantic egotism appears also in *Faust*, and not least in the latter parts of it, which are curiously prophetic. If the hero of that poem has a somewhat incoherent character, soft, wayward, emotional, yet at the same time stubborn and indomitable, that circumstance only renders him the fitter vehicle for absolute Will, a metaphysical entity whose business is to be vigorous and endlessly energetic while remaining perfectly plastic. Faust was at first a scholar, fervid and grubbing, but so confused and impatient that he gave up science for magic. Notwithstanding the shams of professional people which offended him, a private and candid science was possible, which might have brought him intellectual satisfaction; and the fact would not have escaped him if he had been a simple lover of truth. But absolute Will cannot be restricted to any single interest, much less to the pursuit of a frigid truth in which it cannot believe; for the will would not be absolute if it recognized any truth which it had to discover; it can recognize and love only the truth that it makes. Its method of procedure, we are told, consists in first throwing out certain assumptions, such perhaps as that everything must have a cause or that life and progress must be everlasting; and the truth is then whatever conforms to these assumptions. But since evidently these assumptions might be utterly false, it is clear that what interests absolute Will is not truth at all, but only orthodoxy. A delightful illustration of this is given by Faust when, emulating Luther for a moment, he undertakes to translate the first verse of Saint John—that being the Gospel that impresses him most favourably. The point is not prosaically to discover what the Evangelist meant, but rather what he must and shall have meant. *The Word* will never do; *the Sense* would be somewhat better; but *In the beginning was Force* would have even more to recommend it. Suddenly, however, what absolute Will demands flashes upon him, and he writes down contentedly: *In the beginning was the Deed:*

> Auf einmal seh' ich Rat
> Und schreibe getrost; Im Anfang war die That!

Yet even in this exciting form, the life of thought cannot hold him long. He aches to escape from it; not that his knowledge of the sciences, as well as his magic, will not accompany him through life; he will not lose his acquired art nor his habit of reflection, and in this sense his career is really a progress, in that his experience accumulates; but the living interest is always something new. He turns to miscellaneous adventures, not excluding love; from that he passes to imperial politics, a sad mess, thence to sentimental classicism, rather an unreality, and finally to war, to public works, to trade, to piracy, to colonization, and to clearing his acquired estates of tiresome old natives, who insist on ringing church bells and are impervious to the new *Kultur*. These public enterprises he finds more satisfying, perhaps only because he dies in the midst of them.

Are these hints of romantic egotism in Goethe mere echoes of his youth and of the ambient philosophy, echoes which he would have rejected if confronted with them in an abstract and doctrinal form, as he rejected the system of Fichte? Would he not have judged Schopenhauer more kindly? Above all, what would he have thought of Nietzsche, his own wild disciple? No doubt he would have wished to buttress and qualify in a thousand ways that faith in absolute Will which they emphasized so exclusively, Schopenhauer in metaphysics and Nietzsche in morals. But the same faith was a deep element in his own genius, as in that of his country, and he would hardly have disowned it.

CHAPTER V

SEEDS OF EGOTISM IN KANT

KANT is remarkable among sincere philosophers for the pathetic separation which existed between his personal beliefs and his official discoveries. His personal beliefs were mild and half orthodox and hardly differed from those of Leibniz; but officially he was entangled in the subjective criticism of knowledge, and found that the process of knowing was so complicated and so exquisitely contrived to make knowledge impossible, that while the facts of the universe were there, and we might have, like Leibniz, a shrewd and exact notion of what they were, officially we had no right to call them facts or to allege that we knew them. As there was much in Kant's personal belief which this critical method of his could not sanction, so there were implications and consequences latent in his critical method which he never absorbed, being an old man when he adopted it. One of these latent implications was egotism.

The fact that each spirit was confined to its own perceptions condemned it to an initial subjectivity and agnosticism. What things might exist besides his ideas he could never know. That such things existed was not doubted; Kant never accepted that amazing principle of dogmatic egotism that nothing is able to exist unless I am able to know it. On the contrary he assumed that human perceptions, with the moral postulates which he added to them, were symbols of a real world of forces or spirits existing beyond. This assumption reduced our initial idiotism to a constitutional taint of our animal minds, not unlike original sin, and excluded that romantic pride and self-sufficiency in which a full-fledged transcendentalism always abounds.

To this contrite attitude of Kant's agnosticism his personal character and ethics corresponded. A wizened little old bachelor, a sedentary provincial scribe, scrupulous and punctual, a courteous moralist who would have us treat humanity in the person of another as an end and never merely as a means, a pacifist and humanitarian who so revered the moral sense according to Shaftesbury and Adam Smith that, after having abolished earth and heaven, he was entirely comforted by the sublime truth that nevertheless it remained wrong to tell a lie—such a figure has nothing in it of the officious egotist or the superman. Yet his very love of exactitude and his scruples about knowledge, misled by the psychological fallacy that nothing can be an object of knowledge except some idea in the mind, led him in the end to subjectivism; while his rigid conscience, left standing in that unnatural void, led him to attribute absoluteness to what he called the categorical imperative. But this void outside and this absolute oracle within are germs of egotism, and germs of the most virulent species.

The categorical imperative, or unmistakable voice of conscience, was originally something external enough —too external, indeed, to impose by itself a moral obligation. The thunders of Sinai and the voice from the whirlwind in Job fetched their authority from the suggestion of power; there spoke an overwhelming physical force of which we were the creatures and the playthings, a voice which, far from interpreting our sense of justice, or our deepest hopes, threatened to crush and to flout them. If some of its commandments were moral, others were ritual or even barbarous; the only moral sanction common to them all came from our natural prudence and love of life; our wisdom imposed on us the fear of the Lord. The prophets and the Gospel did much to identify this external divine authority with the human conscience; an identification which required a very elaborate theory of sin and punishment and of existence in other worlds, since the actual procedure of nature and history can never be squared with any ideal of right.

In Kant, who in this matter followed Calvin, the independence between the movement of nature, both within and without the soul, and the ideal of right was exaggerated into an opposition. The categorical imperative was always authoritative, but perhaps never obeyed. The divine law was far from being like the absolute Will in Fichte, Hegel, and Schopenhauer, a name for a universal metaphysical force, or even for the flux of material substance. On the contrary the sublimity of the categorical imperative lay precisely in the fact that, while matter and life moved on in their own unregenerate way, a principle which they *ought* to follow, overarched and condemned them, and constrained them to condemn themselves. Human nature was totally depraved and incapable of the least merit, nor had it any power of itself to become righteous. Its amiable spontaneous virtues, having but a natural motive, were splendid vices. Moral worth began only when the will, transformed at the touch of unmerited grace, surrendered every impulse in overwhelming reverence for the divine law.

This Calvinistic doctrine might seem to rebuke all actual inclinations, and far from making the will morally absolute, as egotism would, to raise over against it an alien authority. That which *ought* to be willed. Such was, of course, Kant's ostensible intention; but sublime as such a situation was declared to be, he felt rather dissatisfied in its presence. A categorical imperative crying in the wilderness, a duty which nobody need listen to, or suffer for disregarding, seemed rather a forlorn authority. To save the face of absolute right another world seemed to be required, as in orthodox Christianity, in which it might be duly vindicated and obeyed.

Kant's scepticism, by which all knowledge of reality was denied us, played conveniently into the hands of this pious requirement. If the whole natural world, which we can learn something about by experience, is merely an idea in our minds, nothing prevents any sort of real but unknown world from lying about us unawares. What could be more plausible and opportune than that the categorical imperative which the human mind, the builder of this visible world, had rejected, should in that other real world be the head stone of the corner?

This happy thought, had it stood alone, might have seemed a little fantastic; but it was only a laboured means of re-establishing the theology of Leibniz, in which Kant privately believed, behind the transcendental idealism which he had put forward professorially. The dogmatic system from which he started seemed to him, as it stood, largely indefensible and a little oppressive. To purify it he adopted a fallacious principle of criticism, namely, that our ideas are all we can know, a principle which, if carried out, would undermine that whole system, and every other. He, therefore, hastened to adopt a corrective principle of reconstruction, no less fallacious, namely, that conscience bids us assume certain things to be realities which reason and experience know nothing of. This brought him round to a qualified and ambiguous form of his original dogmas, to the effect that although there was no reason to think that God, heaven, and free-will exist, we ought to act as if they existed, and might call that wilful action of ours faith in their existence.

Thus in the philosophy of Kant there was a stimulating ambiguity in the issue. He taught rather less than he secretly believed, and his disciples, seizing the principle of his scepticism, but lacking his conservative instincts, believed rather less than he taught them. Doubtless in his private capacity Kant hoped, if he did not believe, that God, free-will, and another life subsisted in fact, as every believer had hitherto supposed; it was only the method of proving their reality that had been illegitimate. For no matter how strong the usual arguments might seem (and they did not seem very strong), they could convey no transcendent assurance; on the contrary, the more proofs you draw for anything from reason and experience, the better you prove that that thing is a mere idea in your mind. It was almost prudent, so to speak, that God, freedom, and immortality, if they had claims to reality, should remain without witness in the sphere of 'knowledge,' as inadvertently or ironically it was still called; but to circumvent this compulsory lack of evidence God had at least implanted in us a veridical conscience, which, if it took itself seriously (as it ought to do, being a conscience), would constrain us to postulate what, though we could never 'know' it, happened to be the truth. Such was the way in which the good Kant thought to play hide-and-seek with reality.

The momentum of his transcendental method, however, led to a very different and quite egotistical conclusion. An adept in transcendentalism can hardly suppose that God, free-will, and heaven, even if he postulates them, need exist at all. Existence, for him, is an altogether inferior category. Even a specific moral law, thundering unalterable maxims, must seem to him a childish notion. What the ego postulates is nothing fixed and already existing, but only such ideal terms as, for the moment, express its attitude. If it is striving to remember, it posits a past; if it is planning, it posits a future; if it is consciously eloquent, it posits an audience. These things do not and cannot exist otherwise than in their capacity of things posited by the ego. All, therefore, that the categorical imperative can mean for the complete transcendentalist is that he should live as if all things were real which are imaginatively requisite for him, if he is to live hard: this intensity of life in him being itself the only reality. At that stage of development at which Kant found himself, God, freedom, and immortality may have been necessary postulates of practical reason. But to suppose that these imagined objects, therefore, existed apart from the excellent philosopher whose conscience had not yet transcended them, would be not to have profited by his teaching. It would be merely to repeat it. A later and more advanced transcendentalist, instead of God, freedom, and immortality, might just as dutifully posit matter, empire, and the beauty of a warrior's death. His conscience might no longer be an echo of Christianity, but the trumpet-blast of a new heathenism. It is for the ego who posits to judge what it should posit.

The postulates of practical reason, by which Kant hoped to elude the subjectivity which he attributed to knowledge, are no less subjective than knowledge, and far more private and variable. The senses and the intellect, if they deceive us, seem to deceive us all in much the same way, and the dream they plunge us into in common seems to unite us; but what obscurity, diversity, hostility in the ideals of our hearts! The postulates that were intended to save the Kantian philosophy from egotism are the most egotistical part of it. In the categorical imperative we see something native and inward to the private soul, in some of its moods, quietly claiming to rule the invisible world, to set God on his throne and open eternity to the human spirit. The most subjective of feelings, the feeling of what ought to be, legislates for the universe. Egotism could hardly go further.

But this is not all. The categorical imperative, not satisfied with proclaiming itself secretly omnipotent, proclaims itself openly ruthless. Kant expressly repudiated as unworthy of a virtuous will any consideration of happiness, or of consequences, either to oneself or to others. He was personally as mild and kindly as the Vicar of Wakefield (whose goodness he denied to be moral because it was natural), but his moral doctrine was in principle a perfect frame for fanaticism. Give back, as time was bound to give back, a little flesh to this skeleton of duty, make it the voice not of a remote Mosaic decalogue, but of a rich temperament and a young life, and you will have sanctified beforehand every stubborn passion and every romantic crime. In the guise of an infallible conscience, before which nothing has a right to stand, egotism is launched upon its irresponsible career.

The categorical imperative, as Kant personally conceived it, was that of the conscience of the eighteenth century, which had become humanitarian without ceasing to be Christian, the conscience of the Puritans passing into that of Rousseau. But the categorical principle in morals, like the ego in logic, can easily migrate. If to-day you are right in obeying your private conscience against all considerations of prudence or kindness (though you are prudent and kind by nature, so that this loyalty to a ruthless duty is a sacrifice for you), to-morrow you may be right in obeying the categorical imperative of your soul in another phase, and to carry out no matter what irresponsible enterprise, though your heart may bleed at the victims you are making. The principle of fanaticism is present in either case; and Kant provides, in his transcendental agnosticism, a means of cutting off all protests from experience or common sense, or a more enlightened

50

self-interest. These protests, he thinks, are not only ignoble, but they come from a deluded mind, since the world they regard is a creature of the imagination, whereas the categorical imperative, revealed to the inner man, is a principle prior to all worlds and, therefore, not to be corrected by any suasion which this particular world, now imagined by us, might try to exercise on our free minds.

Thus it is from Kant, directly or indirectly, that the German egotists draw the conviction which is their most tragic error. Their self-assertion and ambition are ancient follies of the human race; but they think these vulgar passions the creative spirit of the universe. Kant, or that soul within Kant which was still somewhat cramped in its expression, was the prophet and even the founder of the new German religion.

CHAPTER VI

TRANSCENDENTALISM PERFECTED

FICHTE purified the system of Kant of all its inconsistent and humane elements; he set forth the subjective system of knowledge and action in its frankest and most radical form. The ego, in order to live a full and free life, posited or feigned a world of circumstances, in the midst of which it might disport itself; but this imagined theatre was made to suit the play, and though it might seem to oppress the Will with all sorts of hindrances, and even to snuff it out altogether, it was really only a mirage which that Will, being wiser than it knew, had raised in order to enjoy the experience of exerting itself manfully.

It would seem obvious from this that the Will could never be defeated, and that in spite of its name it was identical with destiny or the laws of nature: and those transcendentalists who lean to naturalism, or pass into it unawares, like Schelling or Emerson, actually understand the absolute Will in this way. But not so Fichte, nor what I take to be the keener and more heroic romantic school, whose last prophet was Nietzsche. The Germans, in the midst of their fantastic metaphysics, sometimes surprise us by their return to immediate experience: after all, it was in wrestling with the Lord that their philosophy was begotten. As a matter of fact, the Will is often defeated—especially if we are stubborn in defining our will; and this tragic fact by no means refutes the Fichtean philosophy, which knows how to deal with it heroically. It conceives that what is inviolable is only what ought to be, the unconscious plan or idea of perfect living which is hidden in the depths of all life: a will not animated in some measure by this idea cannot exist, or at least cannot be noticed or respected by this philosophy. But when, where, how often and how far this divine idea shall be carried out is left unexplained. Actual will may be feeble or wicked in any degree; and in consequence the world that ought to be evoked in its maximum conceivable richness, may dwindle and fade to nothing.

The Will may accordingly be defeated; not, indeed, by imagined external things, but by its own apathy and tergiversation. In this case, according to the logic of this system (which is as beautifully thought out as that of Plotinus), the dissolving world will appear to be overwhelmingly formidable and real. In expiring because we have no longer the warmth to keep it alive, it will seem to be killing us; for the passivity of the ego, says Fichte, is posited as activity in the non-ego. That way of speaking is scholastic; but the thought, if we take the egotistical point of view, is deep and true.

So any actual will may perish by defect and die out; but actual will may also perish by sublimation. The true object of absolute Will is not things or pleasures or length of life, but willing itself; and the more intense and disinterested this willing is, the better it manifests absolute Will. The heroic act of dashing oneself against overwhelming obstacles may, therefore, be the highest fulfilment of the divine idea. The Will dares to perish in order to have dared everything. In its material ruin it remains ideally victorious. If we consider the matter under the form of eternity, we shall see that this heroic and suicidal will has accomplished what it willed; it has not only lived perilously but perished nobly.

It is hardly necessary to point out how completely this theory justifies any desperate enterprise to which one happens to be wedded. It justifies, for instance, any wilful handling of history and science. The Will by right lays down the principles on which things must and shall be arranged. If things slip somehow from the traces, so much the grander your 'scientific deed' in striving to rein them in. After all, you first summoned them into being only that you might drive them. If they seem to run wild and upset you, like the steeds of Hippolytus, you will, at least, not have missed the glory, while you lived and drove, of assuming the attitude of a master. Call spirits from the vasty deep: if they do not come, what of it? That will only prove the absolute self-sufficiency of your duty to call them.

What tightens this speculative bond between Fichte and the Nietzschean school is that he himself applied his theory of absolute Will to national life. This ego, which was identical with mind in general, he identified also with the German people. If the Germans suffered their national will to be domesticated in the Napoleonic empire, the creative spirit of the universe would be extinguished, and God Himself, who existed only when incarnate in mankind, would disappear. It was evidently one's duty to prevent this if possible; and Fichte poured out all the vehemence of his nature into the struggle for freedom. The mere struggle, the mere protest in the soul, according to his system, would secure the end desired: self-assertion, not material success, was the goal. A happy equilibrium once established in human life would have been only a temptation, a sort of Napoleonic or Mephistophelian quietus falling on the will to strive.

I am not sure how far Fichte, in his romantic and puritan tension of soul, would have relished the present organization of Germany. He was a man of the people, a radical and an agitator as much as a prophet of nationalism, and the shining armour in which German freedom is now encased might have seemed to him too ponderous. He might have discerned in victory the beginning of corruption.

Nevertheless we should remember that a perfected idealism has a tendency to change into its opposite and become a materialism for all practical purposes. Absolute Will is not a natural being, not anybody's will or thought; it is a disembodied and unrealized genius which first comes into operation when it begins to surround itself with objects and points of resistance, so as to become aware of its own stress and vocation. What these objects or felt resistances may be is not prejudged; or rather it is prejudged that they shall be most opposite to spirit, and that spirit shall experience its own passivity—one mode of its fated and requisite experience—in the form of an influence which it imputes to dead and material things.

The whole business of spirit may, therefore, well be with matter. Science might be mechanical, art might be cumbrous and material, all the instruments of life might be brutal, life itself might be hard, bitter, and obsessed, and yet the whole might remain a direct manifestation of pure spirit, absolute freedom, and creative duty. This speculative possibility is worth noting: it helps us to understand modern Germany. It is no paradox that idealists should be so much at home among material things. These material things, according to them, are the offspring of their spirit. Why should they not sink fondly into the manipulation of philological details or chemical elements, or over-ingenious commerce and intrigue? Why should they not dote on blood and iron? Why should these fruits of the spirit be uncongenial to it?

A theoretical materialist, who looks on the natural world as on a soil that he has risen from and feeds on, may perhaps feel a certain piety towards those obscure abysses of nature that have given him birth; but his delight will be rather in the clear things of the imagination, in the humanities, by which the rude forces of nature are at once expressed and eluded. Not so the transcendentalist. Regarding his mind as the source of everything, he is moved to solemn silence and piety only before himself: on the other hand, what bewitches him, what he loves to fondle, is his progeny, the material environment, the facts, the laws, the blood, and the iron in which he conceives (quite truly, perhaps) that his spirit perfectly and freely expresses itself. To despise the world and withdraw into the realm of mind, as into a subtler and more congenial sphere, is quite contrary to his idealism. Such a retreat might bring him peace, and he wants war. His idealism teaches him that strife and contradiction, as Heraclitus said, are the parents of all things; and if he stopped striving, if he grew sick of ambition and material goods, he thinks he would be forsaking life, for he hates as he would death what another kind of idealists have called salvation.

We are told that God, when He had made the world, found it very good, and the transcendentalist, when he assumes the Creator's place, follows His example. The hatred and fear of matter is perhaps not a sign of a pure spirit. Even contemplatively, a divine mind may perfectly well fall in love with matter, as the Moon-goddess did with Endymion. Such matter might be imagined only, as if Diana had merely dreamt of her swain; and the fond image might not be less dear on that account. The romantic poet finds his own spirit greeting him in rocks, clouds, and waves; the musician pours out his soul in movement and tumult; why should not the transcendental general, or engineer, or commercial traveller find his purest ideal in trade, crafts, and wars? Grim work, above all, is what absolute Will demands. It needs the stimulus of resistance to become more intensely conscious of Self, which is said to be its ultimate object in imagining a world at all. Acquisition interests it more than possession, because the sense of effort and power is then more acute. The more material the arts that engage it, and the more complicated and worldly its field of action, the more intense will be its exertion, and the greater its joy. This is no idealism for a recluse or a moping poet; it does not feel itself to be something incidental and fugitive in the world, like a bird's note, that it should fear to be drowned in the crash of material instruments or to be forced to a hideous tension and shrillness: shrillness and tension are its native element. It is convinced that it has composed all the movements there are or can be in existence, and it feels all the more masterful, the more numerous and thunderous is the orchestra it leads. It is entirely at home in a mechanical environment, which it can prove transcendentally to be perfectly ideal. Its most congenial work is to hack its way through to the execution of its World-Plan. Its most adequate and soul-satisfying expression is a universal battle.

CHAPTER VII

FICHTE ON THE MISSION OF GERMANY

WHEN the ancient Jews enlarged their conception of Jehovah so as to recognize in Him the only living God to whom all nature and history were subject, they did not cease to regard the universal power as at the same time their special national deity. Here was a latent contradiction. It was ingeniously removed by saying that Jehovah, while not essentially a tribal deity, had chosen Israel for His people by a free act of grace with no previous merit on their part; so that the pride of the Jews was not without humility.

No humility, however, is mingled with the claim which the Germans now make to a similar pre-eminence. 'Modern critics,' says Max Stirner, 'inveigh against religion because it sets up God, the divine, or the moral law over against man, regarding them as external things, whereas the critics transform all these objects into ideas in the human mind. Nevertheless the essential mistake of religion, to assign a mission to man at all, is not avoided by these critics, who continue to insist that man shall be divine, or ideally human, or what not; morality, freedom, humanity, etc., are his essence.' Now a divinity which is subjective or immanent evidently cannot choose any nation, save by dwelling and manifesting itself more particularly in them. They can be highly favoured only in that they are intrinsically superior, and on that account may be figuratively called vessels of election. Therefore, if the spirit which is in a nation is not one spirit among many in the world (as the primitive Hebrews supposed and as a naturalistic philosophy would maintain), but is the one holy and universal spirit, and if at the same time this spirit dwells in that nation pre - eminently, or even exclusively, humility on the part of this nation would evidently be out of place. Accordingly, the Germans cannot help bearing witness to the divine virtues and prerogatives which they find in themselves, some of which are set forth by Fichte as follows:

The present age stands precisely in the middle of earthly time, between the era in which men were still self-seeking, earthly, and impulsive, and the coming era in which they will live for the sake of pure ideals. The Germans prefigure this better age, and are leading the rest of the world into it. They have created the modern world by uniting the political heritage of classical Europe with the true religion that lingered in Asia, and they have raised the two to a higher unity in their *Kultur*. From them is drawn the best blood of most other nations and the spiritual force that has fashioned them all.

The Germans have never forsaken their native land

nor suffered seriously from immigration. Their language is primitive, and they have never exchanged it for a foreign one. Hence German alone is truly a mother-tongue. Its intellectual terms retain a vital and vivid connection with sensible experience. True poetry and philosophy, therefore, exist only in German. Captious persons who judge by mere crude feeling may fancy that German is not very melodious; but these matters cannot be rightly judged without reference to first principles, which in this case would prove that the sweetest language is that which exhausts all possible sounds and combines them in all available ways. Whether German or some other language comes nearest to this *a priori* ideal of euphony must be left for empirical observation to decide.

The German nature, being pure, deep, earnest, and bold, has instinctively seized upon the true essence of Christianity and discarded with abhorrence all the lies and corruption that obscured it. This essence is the imperative need of turning from the natural to the ideal life. The German knows that his own soul is safe; but this is not enough for him in his unselfishness. His zeal is kindled easily for warmth and light every-where; and this zeal of his is patient and efficacious, taking hold on real life and transforming it. As he presses on he finds more than he sought, for he has plunged into the quick stream of life which forges ahead of itself and carries him forward with it. The dead heart of other nations may dream of gods in the clouds, or of some perfect type of human life already exemplified in the past and only to be approached or repeated in the future. The spirit of the German is no coinage of earth; it is the living source of all the suns, and rushes to create absolutely new things for ever. The German mind is the self-consciousness of God.

I do not see that the strain of war or the intoxication of victory could add much to these boasts, uttered by Fichte when, for the moment, he had abandoned all hope of military self-assertion on the part of his country, and relied on education and philosophy alone to preserve and propagate German righteousness. Even in detail, what he says often seems strangely like what official Germany is now saying. Even the hysterical hatred of England is not absent. In England Fichte did not see the champion of Protestantism, morality, and political liberty, nor the constant foe of Napoleon, but only a universal commercial vampire. His contempt for the Latin races, too, was boundless. In the matter of race, indeed, he entertained a curious idea that there must have been, from all eternity until the beginning of history, a primitive Normal People, a tribe of Adams and Eves, because according to a principle which he adopted from Calvinistic theology, if all men had been originally slaves to nature none could ever have become free. This normal people were, of course, the ancestors of the Germans. Earth-born savage tribes must have

existed also for the normal people to subdue, since but
for some such conquest the primitive equilibrium would
never have been broken, Eden and the jungle would
never have been merged together, and history, which is
a record of novelties, would never have begun. The
theory of evolution has rendered the reasons for such a
view obsolete; but the idea that the bulk of mankind
are mongrels formed by the union of blond god-like
creatures with some sort of anthropoid blacks, recurred
later in Gobineau and has had a certain vogue in Germany.

Fichte, following Calvin and Kant, made a very
sharp distinction between the life of nature and that
of duty. The ideal must be pursued without the
least thought of advantage. Trades, he says, must be
practised spontaneously, without any other reward
than longer vigils. The young must never hear it
mentioned that any one could ever be incited or guided
in life by the thought of his own preservation or well-
being. Knowledge is no report of existing things or
laws which have happened to be discovered. Knowledge is the very life of God, and self-generated. It is
'an intellectual activity for its own sake, according to
rules for their own sake.' In plain English, it is pure
imagination. But the method to be imposed on this
madness is fixed innately, both for thought and for
morals. Only frivolity can interfere with a unanimous
idealism.

We must not suppose that this prescription of austere and abstract aims implies any aversion on Fichte's part to material progress, compulsory *Kultur*, or military conquest. German idealism, as we have seen, is not Platonic or ascetic, that it should leave the world behind. On the contrary, its mission is to consecrate the world and show that every part of it is an organ of the spirit. This is a form of piety akin to the Hebraic. Even the strictest Calvinists, who taught that the world was totally depraved, were able, in every sense of the phrase, to make a very good thing of it. They reclaimed, they appropriated, they almost enjoyed it. So Fichte gives us prophetic glimpses of an idealistic Germany conquering the world. The State does not aim at self-preservation, still less is it concerned to come to the aid of those members of the human family that lag behind the movement of the day. The dominion of unorganized physical force must be abolished by a force obedient to reason and spirit. True life consists in refashioning human relations after a model innate in the mind. The glorious destiny of Germany is to bring forth and establish the world anew. Natural freedom is a disgraceful thing, a mere medley of sensual and intellectual impulses without any principle of order. It is for the Germans to decide whether a providential progress exists by becoming themselves the providence that shall bring progress about, or whether on the contrary every higher thought is folly. If they should fail, history would never blame them, for in that case there would be no more history.

The sole animating principle of history is the tendency towards a universal Christian European monarchy. This tendency is deeper than the plans of men and stronger than their intentions. 'That a State, even when on the very point of making war, should solemnly assert its love of peace and its aversion to conquest, is nothing; for in the first place it must needs make this asseveration and so hide its real intention if it would succeed in its design; and the well-known principle *Threaten war that thou mayst have peace* may also be inverted in this way: *Promise peace that thou mayst begin war with advantage*; and in the second place the State may be wholly in earnest in its peaceful assurances, so far as its self-knowledge has gone; but let the favourable opportunity for aggrandizement present itself, and the previous good resolution is forgotten.'

If the people are disinclined to obey the Idea, the Government must constrain them to do so. All the powers of all the citizens must be absorbed in the State. Personal liberty could be turned to no good use when such individuality and variety of training as are good for the State have been provided for by its regulations. Nor must any idleness be tolerated. An ideal education must make men over so that they shall be incapable of willing anything but what that education wills them to will. The State may then rely upon its subjects, 'for whoever has a well-grounded will, wills what he wills for all eternity.'

As to foreign relations, the State, in obedience to its ideal mission, must conquer the surrounding barbarians and raise them to a state of culture. It is this process almost exclusively that has introduced progress into history. 'What impels the Macedonian hero . . . to seek foreign lands? What chains victory to his footsteps and scatters before him in terror the countless hordes of his enemies? Is this mere fortune? No; it is an Idea. . . . The civilized must rule and the uncivilized must obey, if right is to be the law of the world. . . . Tell me not of the thousands who fell round his path; speak not of his own early death. After the realization of his idea, what was there greater for him to do than to die?'

This enthusiasm for Alexander (which Hegel shared) is not merely retrospective. 'At last in one nation of the world the highest, purest morality, such as was never seen before among men, will arise and will be made secure for all future time, and thence will be extended over all other peoples. There will ensue a transformation of the human race from earthly and sensual creatures into pure and noble spirits.' 'Do you know anything higher than death? . . . Who has a right to stand in the way of an enterprise begun in the face of this peril?'

It may seem curious that an uncompromising

puritan like Fichte, a prophet sprung from the people, a theoretical republican who quarrelled with his students for forming clubs and fighting duels, a fierce idealist full of contempt for worldlings, should have so perfectly supplied the Junkers and bankers with their philosophy. But the phenomenon is not new. Plato, divine and urbane as he was, supplied the dull Spartans with theirs. Men of idealistic faith are confident that the foundations of things must be divine, and when, upon investigating these foundations, they came upon sinister principles— blind impulse, chance, murderous competition—they fanatically erect these very principles into sacred maxims. All strength, they are antecedently convinced, must come from God; therefore if deception, wilfulness, tyranny, and big battalions are the means to power. they must be the chosen instruments of God on earth. In some such way the Catholic Church, too, for fear of impiety, is seen blessing many a form of deceit and oppression. Thus the most ardent speculation may come to sanction the most brutal practice. The primitive passions so sanctioned, because they seem to be safe and potent, are probably too narrowly organized to sustain themselves long; and meantime they miss and trample down the best things that mankind possesses. Nevertheless they are a force like any other, a force not only vehement but contagious, and capable of many victories though of no stable success. Such passions, and the philosophies that glorify them, are sincere, absorbing, and if frankly expressed irrefutable.

The transcendental theory of a world merely imagined by the ego, and the will that deems itself absolute, are certainly desperate delusions; but not more desperate or deluded than many another system that millions have been brought to accept. The thing bears all the marks of a new religion. The fact that the established religions of Germany are still forms of Christianity may obscure the explicit and heathen character of the new faith: it passes for a somewhat faded speculation, or for the creed of a few extremists, when in reality it dominates the judgment and conduct of the nation. No religious tyranny could be more complete. It has its prophets in the great philosophers and historians of the last century; its high priests and pharisees in the Government and the professors; its faithful flock in the disciplined mass of the nation; its heretics in the Socialists; its dupes in the Catholics and the Liberals, to both of whom the national creed, if they understood it, would be an abomination; it has its martyrs now by the million, and its victims among unbelievers are even more numerous, for its victims, in some degree, are all men.

CHAPTER VIII

THE EGOTISM OF IDEAS

WHEN we are discussing egotism need we speak of Hegel? The tone of this philosopher, especially in his later writings, was full of contempt for everything subjective: the point of view of the individual, his opinions and wishes, were treated as of no account unless they had been brought into line with the providential march of events and ideas in the great world. This realism, pronounced and even acrid as it was, was still idealistic in the sense that the substance of the world was conceived to be not material but conceptual—a law or logic which animated phenomena and was the secret of their movement. The world was like a riddle or confused oracle; and the solution to the puzzle lay in the romantic instability or self-contradiction inherent in every finite form of being, which compelled it to pass into something different. The direction of this movement we might understand sympathetically in virtue of a sort of vital dialectic or dramatic necessity in our own reflection. Hegel was a solemn sophist: he made discourse the key to reality.

This technical realism in Hegel was reinforced by

his historical imagination, which continually produces an impression of detachment, objectivity, and impersonal intelligence; he often seems to be lost in the events of his story and to be plucking the very heart out of the world. Again, he adored the State, by which in his view the individual should be entirely subjugated, not for the benefit of other individuals (that would be a sort of vicarious selfishness no less barren than private profit), but in the rapt service of common impersonal ends.

The family was a first natural group in which the individual should be happy to lose himself, the trade-guild was another, and the State was the highest and most comprehensive of all; there was nothing worthy or real in a man except his functions in society.

Nevertheless this denial of egotism is apparent only. It is a play within the play. On the smaller stage the individual—save for his lapses and stammerings—is nothing but the instrument and vehicle of divine decrees; in fact he is a puppet, and the only reality of him is the space he fills in the total spectacle. But that little stage is framed in by another, often overlooked, but ever present; and on this larger and nearer stage the ego struts alone. It is I that pull the strings, enjoy the drama, supply its plot and moral, and possess the freedom and actuality which my puppets lack. On the little stage the soul of a man is only one of God's ideas, and his whole worth lies in helping out the pantomime; on the big stage, God is simply my idea of God and the purpose of the play is to express my mind. The spectacle in which every individual dances automatically to the divine tune is only my dream.

The philosophy of Hegel is accordingly subjective and all its realism is but a pose and a tone wilfully assumed. That this is the truth of the matter might be inferred, apart from many continual hints and implications, from the fact that the system is transcendental and founded on Kant. Objectivity can, therefore, be only a show, a matter of make-believe, something imputed to things and persons by the mind, whose poetic energies it manifests. Everything must be set down as a creation of mind, simply because it is an object of thought or knowledge.

This underlying subjectivism also explains the singular satisfaction of Hegel, whose glance was comprehensive enough, with so strangely limited a world as he describes to us. He described what he knew best or had heard of most, and felt he had described the universe. This illusion was inevitable, because his principle was that the universe was created by description and resided in it. The mission of Hegel, as he himself conceived it, was not to discover the real world or any part of it: in theory he retracted all belief in a real world and set in its place his conception or knowledge of it—therefore quite adequate to its object. If China was the oldest country he had heard of, the world began with China, and if Prussia was the youngest and he (as he had to be) its latest philosopher, the world ended with Prussia and with himself. This seems a monstrous egotism, but it is not arbitrary; in one sense it was the least pretentious of attitudes, since it was limited to the description of a current view, not of a separate or prior object. The value of a philosophy could lie only in the fullness and fidelity with which it might focus the conceptions of the age in which it arose. Hegel hoped to do this for his own times; he did not covet truth to anything further.

The same attitude explains the servility of his moral philosophy, which is simply an apology for the established order of things and for the prejudices of his time and country. His deepest conviction was that no system of ethics could be more, and if it tried to be more would be less, because it would be merely personal. When, for instance, he condemned harshly the Roman *patria potestas* it was because it offended the individualism of the Protestant and modern conscience; and if in the next breath he condemned even more harshly the sentimentalists who made tender feeling and good intentions the test of virtue, it was because these individual consciences absolved themselves from conformity to the established Church and State. To inquire whether in itself or in respect to human economy generally, the morality of Buddha, or Socrates, or Rousseau was the best would have seemed to him absurd: the question

73

could only be what approaches or contributions each of these made to the morality approved by the Lutheran community and by the Prussian ministry of education and public worship. The truth, then as now, was whatever every good German believed. This pious wish of Hegel's to interpret the orthodoxy of his generation was successful, and the modest hopes of his philosophy were fulfilled. Never perhaps was a system so true to its date and so false to its subject.

The egotism of Hegel appears also in his treatment of mathematical and physical questions. The infinite he called the false infinite, so as to avoid the dilemmas which it placed him in, such as why the evolution of the Idea began six thousand years ago, or less; what more could happen now that in his self-consciousness that evolution was complete; why it should have gone on in this planet only, or if it had gone on elsewhere also, why the Idea evolving there might not have been a different Idea. But all such questions are excluded when one understands that this philosophy is only a point of view: the world it describes is a vista not separable from the egotistical perspectives that frame it in. The extent of the world need not be discussed, because that extent is an appearance only; in reality the world has no extent, because it is only my present idea.

The infinite thus lost its application; but the word was too idealistic to be discarded. Accordingly the title of true infinite was bestowed on the eventual illusion of completeness, on an alleged system of relations out of relation to anything beyond. That nothing existent, unless it was the bad infinite, could be absolute in this manner did not ruffle Hegel, for the existent did not really concern him but only 'knowledge,' that is, a circle of present and objectless ideas. Knowledge, however limited in fact, always has the completeness in question for the egotist, whose objects are not credited with existing beyond himself. Egotism could hardly receive a more radical expression than this: to declare the ego infinite because it can never find anything that is beyond its range.

The favourite tenet of Hegel that everything involves its opposite is also a piece of egotism; for it is equivalent to making things conform to words, not words to things; and the ego, particularly in philosophers, is a nebula of words. In defining things, if you insist on defining them, you are constrained to define them by their relation to other things, or even exclusion of them. If, therefore, things are formed by your definitions of them, these relations and exclusions will be the essence of things. The notion of such intrinsic relativity in things is a sophism even in logic, since elementary terms can never be defined yet may be perfectly well understood and arrested in intuition; but what here concerns us is rather the egotistical motive behind that sophism: namely, that the most verbal and subjective accidents to

75

which the names of things are subject in human discourse should be deputed to be the groundwork of the things and their inmost being.

Egotistical, too, was Hegel's tireless hatred of what he called the abstract understanding. In his criticisms of this faculty and the opinions it forms there is much keenness and some justice. People often reason in the abstract, floating on words as on bladders: in their knowingness they miss the complexity and volume of real things. But the errors or abuses into which verbal intelligence may fall would never produce that implacable zeal with which Hegel persecutes it. What obsesses him is the fear that, in spite of its frivolity, the understanding may some day understand; that it may correct its inadequacies, trace the real movement of things, and seeing their mechanism lose that *effet d'ensemble*, that dramatic illusion, which he calls reason.

Imagine a landscape-painter condemned to have a naturalist always at his elbow: soon it would not be merely the errors of the naturalist that would irritate him, but the naturalist himself. The artist intent on panoramic effects does not wish to be forced to look through a microscope; in changing his focus he loses his subjective object: not reality but appearance is the reality for him. Hegel, since it was his mission to substitute so-called knowledge for being, had to go further; he had to convince himself, not only that the structure of nature discovered by the understanding was irrelevant to his own conceptual mythology, but that such a structure did not exist. He was not willing to confess (as the landscape-painter might) that he *was* an egotist; that it was the subjective that interested him, and that in so great a world the subjective too has its place. No! he must pretend that his egotism was not egotism, but identity with the absolute, and that those who dared to maintain that the world wagged in its own way, apart from the viewing mind, were devils, because they suggested that the viewing mind was not God.

It is this latent but colossal egotism that makes plausible the strange use which Hegel sometimes makes of the word substance. His substance is but his grammar of discourse; for he was not looking for substance, in which he could not consistently believe, but only for the ultimate synthetic impression which he might gather from appearances. For the theatre-goer, the function of scenery and actors is that they should please and impress him: but what, in the end, impresses and pleases him? The cumulative burden and force of the play; the enhanced life which it has stimulated in himself. This, for that ruthless egotist, the aesthete, is the *substance* of all things theatrical. Of course, in fact, nothing could be falser, for the author and actors are real people, with lives far outrunning their function in the theatre and truly grounding it. Even the stage machinery has its natural history, and the artisans who made it have theirs, both full of mute inglorious tragedies. These real substances behind his entertainment the spectator, in his aesthetic egotism, laughs at as irrelevant; for him, as for Hamlet, the play's the thing. What is most his own, his imaginative reaction on the spectacle, the terms in which he finds it easiest and most exciting to describe it, he calls the substance of it: a term which betrays the profound impudence of the deliberate egotist; the deepest reality he will recognize is merely specious, existing only for the mind that imagines it. What is supposed to rescue the system of Hegel from subjectivism is the most subjective of things—a dialectic which obeys the impulses of a theoretical *parti pris*, and glorifies a fixed idea.

When we have understood all this, those traits of Hegel's which at first sight seem least egotistical—his historical insight and his enthusiasm for organized society—take on a new colour. That historical insight is not really sympathetic; it is imperious, external, contemptuous, feigned. If you are a modern reading the Greeks, especially if you read them in the romantic spirit of Goethe's classicism, and know of them just what Hegel knew, you will think his description wonderfully penetrating, masterly, and complete: but would Aeschylus or Plato have thought it so? They would have laughed, or rather they would not have understood that such a description referred to them at all. It is the legend of the Greeks, not the life of the Greeks, that is analysed by him. So his account of medieval religion represents the Protestant legend, not the Catholic experience. What we know little or nothing about seems to us in Hegel admirably characterized: what we know intimately seems to us painted with the eye of a pendantic, remote, and insolent foreigner. It is but an idea of his own that he is foisting upon us, calling it our soul. He is creating a world in his head which might be admirable, if God had made it.

Every one is subject to such illusions of perspective and to the pathos of distance, now favourable, now unfavourable to what he studies; but Hegel, thinking he had the key to the divine design, fancied himself deeply sympathetic because he saw in everything some fragment of himself. But no part of the world was that; every part had its own inalienable superiority, which to transcend was to lose for ever. To the omniscient egotist every heart is closed. The past will never give away its secret except to some self-forgetful and humble lover who by nature has a kindred destiny. The egotist who thinks to grasp it, so as to serve it up at his philosophic banquet, or exhibit it in his museum of antiquities, grasps only himself; and in that sense, to his confusion, his egotism turns out true.

The egotism that appears in this lordly way of treating the past is egotism of the imagination, the same that was expressed in the romantic love of nature, which was really a very subtle, very studious, very obstinate love of self, intent on finding some reference and deference to oneself in everything. But there is also an egotism of passion, which in Hegel appears in his worship of the state. 'The passions' is the old and fit name for what the Germans call ideals. The passions are not selfish in the sense in which the German moralists denounce selfishness; they are not contrived by him who harbours them for his ulterior profit. They are ideal, dangerous, often fatal. Even carnal passions are not selfish, if by the self we understand the whole man: they are an obsession to which he sacrifices himself. But the transcendental philosophy with its migratory ego can turn any single passion, or any complex of passions, into a reputed centre of will, into a moral personage. As the passion usurps more and more of the man's nature it becomes a fierce egotist in his place; it becomes fanaticism or even madness.

This substitution of a passion for a man, when nobody thought the ego migratory, seemed a disease. What folly, we said to the human soul, to sacrifice your natural life to this partial, transitory, visionary passion! But the German idealist recognises no natural life, no natural individual. His ego can migrate into any political body or any synthetic idea. Therefore, his passions, far from seeming follies to him, seem divine inspirations, calls to sacrifice, fidelities to the ideal.

I am far from wishing to say that a German idealist

is commonly just to all the passions and raises them in turn to be his highest and absolute will. His passions are generally few and mental. Accidents of training or limitations of temperament keep him respectable; but he is never safe. Dazzle him with a sophism, such, for instance, as that 'the more evil the more good,' or hypnotize him with a superstition, such as that 'organization is an end in itself,' and nothing more is needed to turn him into a romantic criminal.

Even the absolute requires an enemy to whet its edge upon, and the State, which according to Hegel is morally absolute, requires rival states in order that its separate individuality may not seem to vanish, and with it the occasion for blessed and wholesome wars. Hegel rejects the notion that nations have any duties to one another because, as he asserts, there is no moral authority or tribunal higher than the State, to which its government could be subject. This assertion is evidently false, since in the first place there is God or, if the phrase be preferred, there is the highest good of mankind, hedging in very narrowly the path that states should follow between opposite vices; and in the second place there is the individual, whose natural allegiance to his family, friends, and religion, to truth and to art, is deeper and holier than his allegiance to the State, which for the soul of man is an historical and geographical accident. No doubt at the present stage of civilization there is more to be gained than lost by co-operating loyally with the governments under which we happen to live, not because any state is divine, but because as yet no less cumbrous machinery is available for carrying on the economy of life with some approach to decency and security. For Hegel, however, the life of the State was the moral substance, and the souls of men but the accidents; and as to the judgment of God, he asserted that it was none other than the course of history. This is a characteristic saying, in which he seems to proclaim the moral government of the world, when in truth he is sanctifying a brutal law of success and succession. The best government, of course, succumbs in time like the worst, and sooner; the dark ages followed upon the Roman Empire and lasted twice as long. But Hegel's God was simply the world, or a formula supposed to describe the world. He despised every ideal not destined to be realized on earth, he respected legality more than justice, and extant institutions more than moral ideals; and he wished to flatter a government in whose policy war and even crime were recognized weapons.

This reign of official passion is not, let me repeat, egotism in the natural man who is subject to it; it is the sacrifice of the natural man and of all men to an abstract obsession, called an ideal. The vice of absoluteness and egotism is transferred to that visionary agent. The man may be docile and gentle enough, but the demon he listens to is ruthless and deaf. It forbids him to ask,

'At what price do I pursue this ideal? How much harm must I do to attain this good?' No; this imperative is categorical. The die is cast, the war against human nature and happiness is declared, and an idol that feeds on blood, the Absolute State, is set up in the heart and over the city.

CHAPTER IX

EGOTISM AND SELFISHNESS

IN a review of egotism in German philosophy it would hardly be excusable to ignore the one notable writer who has openly adopted egotism in name as well as in fact. The work of Max Stirner on the single separate person and what he may call his own hardly belongs to German philosophy as I have been using the words: it lacks the transcendental point of departure, as well as all breadth of view, metaphysical subtlety, or generous afflatus; it is a bold, frank, and rather tiresome protest against the folly of moral idealism, against the sacrifice of the individual to any ghostly powers such as God, duty, the State, humanity, or society; all of which this redoubtable critic called 'spooks' and regarded as fixed ideas and pathological obsessions. This crudity was relieved by a strong mother-wit and a dogged honesty; and it is not impossible that this poor schoolmaster, in his solitary meditations, may have embodied prophetically a rebellion against polite and religious follies which is brewing in the working classes—classes which to-morrow perhaps will absorb all mankind and give for the first time a plebeian tone to philosophy.

Max Stirner called the migratory ego back to its nest. He exorcized that 'spook' which had been ascending and descending the ladder of abstractions, lodged now in a single passion, now in a political body, now in a logical term, now in the outspread universe. The only true ego, he insisted, was the bodily person, the natural individual who is born and dies. No other organ or seat existed for the mind, or for any of its functions. Personal interests were the only honest interests a man could have, and if he was browbeaten or indoctrinated into sacrificing them, that moral coercion was a scandal and a wrong. The indomitable individual should shake off those chains, which were only cobwebs, and come into his own.

Egotism thus becomes individualism, and threatens to become selfishness. The logic of these positions does not seem to have been clear to Max Stirner. That the individual must *possess* all his wishes and aspirations, even the most self-denying and suicidal, is obvious; he is the seat of those very obsessions and superstitions which Max Stirner deplored. The same thing is true of knowledge: a man can know only what *he* knows and what his faculties make him capable of knowing. This fact is the excuse for transcendentalism, and the element of truth in it. But the fact that volition and knowledge must have their seat in some person prejudges nothing about the scope of their objects. The fallacy of egotism begins with the inference that, therefore, a person can know only his ideas and can live only for his own benefit. On the contrary, what makes knowledge knowledge is that our sensibility may report something which is not merely our feeling; and our moral being arises when our interests likewise begin to range over the world. To deny that a man is capable of generosity because his generosity must be his own, is insufferable quibbling.

Even our vanities and follies are disinterested in their way; their egotism is not a calculated selfishness. When a man orders his tomb according to his taste, it is not in the hope of enjoying his residence in it.

Max Stirner, while deprecating all subordination of the individual to society, expected people, even after they were emancipated, to form voluntary unions for specific purposes, such as playing games. Did he think that such companionship and co-operation would go without gregarious feelings and ideal interests? Would not a player wish his side to win? Would he not impose a rather painful strain upon himself at times for the sake of that 'spook,' victory? All the sacrifices that society or religion imposes on a man, when they are legitimate, are based on the same principle.

The protest of Max Stirner against sham ideals and aims forced upon us by social pressure should not then have extended to ideals congenial to the natural man and founded on his instincts. Since the seat of our enthusiasms must be personal, their appeal should be so too, if they are to inspire us efficaciously; but every

art and science shows that they may be utterly impersonal in their object. It was not in proposing ideal
aims that the German philosophers were wrong: that
was the noble and heroic side of their doctrine, as well
as a point in which their psychology was correct. Their
error lay in defining these aims arbitrarily and imposing
them absolutely, trying to thrust into us ideals like
endless strife and absolute will, which perhaps our
souls abhor. But if our souls abhor those things, it is
because they love something else; and this other thing
they love for its own sake, so that the very refusal to
sacrifice to those idols is a proof of faith in a true God.

The conclusion of Max Stirner, that because those
idols are false, and the worship of them is cruel and
superstitious, therefore we must worship nothing and
merely enjoy in a piggish way what we may call our own,
is a conclusion that misreads human nature. It over-
looks the fact that man lives by the imagination, that
the imagination—when not chaotic and futile—is exercised in the arts of life, that the objects of these arts are
impersonal, and that to achieve these objects brings us a
natural happiness.

The Germans are by nature a good stolid people,
and it is curious that their moralists, of every school,
are so fantastic and bad. The trouble lies perhaps in
this, that they are all precipitate. They have not taken
the trouble to decipher human nature, which is an
endowment, something many-sided, unconscious, with a

margin of variation, and have started instead with the will, which is only an *attitude*, something casual, conscious, and narrowly absolute. Nor have they learned to respect sufficiently the external conditions under which human nature operates and to which it must conform—God, the material world, the nature and will of other men. Their morality consequently terminates in ideals, casual, conscious, and absolute expressions of the passions, or else expires in a mysticism which renounces all moral judgment. A reasonable morality terminates instead in the arts, by which human ideals and passions are compounded with experience and adapted to the materials they must work in. The immaturity of the German moralists appears in their conception that the good is life, which is what an irrational animal might say: whereas for a rational being the good is only the good part of life, that healthy, stable, wise, kind, and beautiful sort of life which he calls happiness.

CHAPTER X

THE BREACH WITH CHRISTIANITY

GERMAN philosophy has a religious spirit, but its alliance with Christianity has always been equivocal and external. Even in the speculations of Leibniz, concerned as he was about orthodoxy, there was a spirit of independence and absolutism which was rationalistic, not to say heathen. The principle of sufficient reason, for instance, demands that God and nature shall explain their existence and behaviour to us, as timid parents explain their behaviour to their censorious children. By rendering everything necessary, even the acts of God, it takes the place of God and makes Him superfluous. Such frigid optimism as this principle involves, besides being fatalistic, is deeply discouraging to that hope of deliverance which is the soul of Christianity: for if this is the best world possible, how poor must be that realm of possible worlds where everything is tainted, and there is no heaven! The theory, too, that each soul contains the seeds of its whole experience and suffices for its own infinite development, destroys the meaning of creation, revelation, miracles, sin, grace, and charity. Thus without intending it, even the obsequious but incredibly intelligent Leibniz undermined all the doctrines of Christianity in the act of thinking them afresh, and insinuated into them a sort of magic heathen individualism.

Kant, Fichte, and Hegel were less punctilious in their theology, but they still intended to be or to seem Christians. They felt that what made the sanctity of traditional religion and its moral force could be recovered in a purer form in their systems. This feeling of theirs was not unwarranted; at least, many religious minds, after the first shock of losing their realistic faith, have seen in transcendentalism a means, and perhaps the only safe means, of still maintaining a sort of Christianity which shall not claim any longer to be a miraculous or exceptional revelation, but only a fair enough poetic symbol for the principles found in all moral life. That he who loses his life shall save it, for instance, is a maxim much prized and much glossed by Hegelians. They lend it a meaning of their own, which might, indeed, be said to be the opposite of what the Gospel meant; for there the believer is urged to discard the very world with which Hegel asks him to identify himself. The idea is that if you surrender your private interests to those of your profession, science, or country, you become thereby a good and important person, and unintentionally a happy one. You will then feel that the world shares your thoughts and renders them perpetual, while you, being absorbed in ideal pursuits, forget your private miseries and mortality.

In this sort of moral psychology there is evidently some truth; but the 'law of experience' which it points to is but a loose and ambiguous law, which disguises more facts than it expresses. Honest minds will rebel against the suggestion that when you outgrow a desire you have fulfilled it; and they will detect the furtive irony in bidding you live hard in order not to feel the vanity of living. To drown sorrow in work, and to forget private failures in public interests, is certainly possible, but it is only drugging yourself with hurry and routine, which may not be more advantageous to others than it really is to yourself. Impersonal or 'ideal' aims are not necessarily less delusive or 'higher' than personal ones; in fact there is far more likelihood that they are conventional humbug. This pathological hygiene of idealism, which always stops at some uncriticized impulse, thinks it secures health when perhaps it has only increased the dose of illusion.

Nevertheless transcendentalism has this important element in common with Christianity and with the other Hebraic religions, that it regards human interests as the core of the universe and God as the God of man, who disposes all things for man's benefit. In its eyes the sphere of providence and moral life is bounded by the history of a part of Europe and Asia for a few thousand years. So long as transcendentalism is taken to imply some such philosophy of history it can compound its differences with liberal Christianity, since they are at one in the cardinal point of their faith, which is the apotheosis of the human spirit.

Yet this human egotism, which comforts so many minds, offends others, in their way no less religious. Of course, those who believe in the infinity of the universe, be they mystics or naturalists, smile at such pettiness and fatuity. But even among transcendentalists, some are repelled; for the dominion which they attribute to their ego is a dominion over appearances only; they do not pretend that the grammar of the human intellect can lay down the law for the world at large. At the same time, in their own house they wish to keep their freedom. That prescribed evolution and that reversible optimism of the absolute transcendentalists are repulsive to them; they resent that such a precise and distasteful career should be imposed on their transcendental individuality, and should swallow it up. It is these rebels that have carried romanticism and German philosophy into its last phase. They have broken at last with Christianity and at the same time with the theological and cosmic transcendentalism that was its treacherous ally, and hoped to be its heir.

The transcendentalism of Schopenhauer, sweeping as it was in its way, retained the modest and agnostic character it had had in Kant: he proclaimed that the world was his idea, but meant only (what is undeniable) that his *idea* of the world was his idea. The egotistical doctrine that the whole universe is but the image of it

92

created by the mind disappeared altogether in his system. The so-called Will which he still placed behind everything was no longer his own will evolving experience out of nothing; it was a fanciful name for whatever force or substance might lie behind experience, animating all its objects, determining their inherent life, and constituting them facts collateral with himself. If his metaphysics remained idealistic, it was on account of his romantic habit of assimilating the life of nature to that of man, as hasty introspection reveals it; so that the universe is described in moral and poetical terms rather than in the terms of science.

The consequences of this change were important. The Will became infinite in what Hegel called the evil sense, that is, in the true one. It was no longer possible to speak of a plan of creation, nor of a dramatic progress in history, with its beginning in Eden and its end in Berlin. Life was seen to radiate, as it really does, from an elementary form into all sorts of disparate and incomparable growths, capable of endless diversity. No limit, no forced co-operation, no stereotyped method was imputed to life. The pocket universe of Hegel opened out to the stars, so hateful to that philosopher. Man lost his importance and at the same time the insufferable burden of his false pretensions. In Schopenhauer frankness returned, and with frankness clearness. Yet he could not quite reconcile man to his actual place in nature. A deep prejudice still intervened.

Both Christianity and romanticism had accustomed people to disregard the intrinsic value of things. Things ought to be useful for salvation, or symbols of other greater but unknown things: it was not to be expected that they should be simply good in themselves. This life was to be justified, if justified at all, only as servile work or tedious business may be justified, not as health or artistic expression justify themselves. Unless some external and ulterior end could be achieved by living, it was thought that life would be vanity. Remove now the expectation of a millennium or of a paradise in the sky, and it may seem that all serious value has disappeared from our earthly existence. Yet this feeling is only a temporary after-image of a particular education.

The romantic poets, through pride, restlessness, and longing for vague impossible things, came to the same conclusion that the Church had reached through censoriousness and hope. To be always dissatisfied seemed to that Faust-like age a mark of loftiness. To be dissatisfied is, indeed, a healthy and promising thing, when what troubles us can be set right; but the romantic mind despises such incidental improvements, which, far from freeing the wild egotistical soul, would rather fatten and harness it. It is beneath the romantic pessimist to remember that people, in all ages, sometimes achieve what they have set their hearts on, and that if human will and conduct were better disciplined, this contentment would be more frequent and more massive. On the contrary, he asserts that willing is always and everywhere abortive.

How can he persuade himself of something so evidently false? By that mystical misinterpretation of human nature which is perhaps the core of romanticism. He imagines that what is desired is not this or that—food, children, victory, knowledge, or some other specific goal of a human instinct—but an abstract and perpetual happiness behind all these alternating interests. Of course an abstract and perpetual happiness is impossible, not merely because events are sure to disturb any equilibrium we may think we have established in our lives, but for the far more fundamental reason that we have no abstract and perpetual instinct to satisfy. The desire for self-preservation or power or union with God is no more perpetual or comprehensive than any other: it is commonly when we are in straits that we become aware of such objects, and to achieve them, or imagine we achieve them, will give us only a momentary satisfaction, like any other success. A highest good to be obtained apart from each and every specific interest is more than unattainable; it is unthinkable. The romanticist, chasing wilfully that *ignis fatuus*, naturally finds his life arduous and disappointing. But he might have learned from Plato or any sound moralist, if his genius could allow him to learn anything, that the highest good of man is the sum and harmony of those specific goods upon which his nature is directed. But because the romantic will was unteachable, all will was declared to be foolish.

Schopenhauer was led into his pessimism also by the spirit of opposition; his righteous wrath was aroused by the sardonic and inhuman optimism of Hegel, the arguments for which were so cogent, so Calvinistic, and so irrelevant that they would have lost none of their force if they had been proposed in hell. The best possible world and the worst possible were, indeed, identical for that philosophy. Schopenhauer needed to change nothing in the description of life, as the other idealists conceived it, in order to prove that life was a tragedy; for they were as romantic as himself and as far from feeling the intrinsic value of happiness, and the possibility of real progress. Real progress has little to do with perpetual evolution. It occurs only in certain places and times, when nature or art comes to the assistance of some definite interest already embodied, as the interest in security and mutual confidence, knowledge, or the fine arts is already embodied in mankind. Schopenhauer was not insensible to these achievements; he felt by instinct the infinity and luxuriance of the moral world. It was in part this secret sympathy with nature that alienated him from Christianity and from transcendental metaphysics. But because natural goods cannot be desired or possessed for ever, he thought their value was cancelled, even for those who desired and possessed them. The leaven of romanticism was still at work, forbidding him to recognize a natural order, with which a vital harmony might be established. The ground of life, the will in all things, was something lurid and tempestuous, itself a psychological chaos. The alternative to theism in the mind of Schopenhauer was not naturalism but anarchy.

This romantic travesty of life and this conception of metaphysical anarchy were inherited by Nietzsche and regarded by him as the last word of philosophy. But he made the breach with Christianity still wider. The grief of Schopenhauer in the presence of such a world, his desperate and exotic remedy—the denial of the will—and his love of contemplation were all evidences of a mind still half Christian: his pessimism itself was so much homage to the faith he had lost. Such backward glances were not for the impetuous Nietzsche, who felt he was a prophet of the future, and really was one. Romantic anarchy delighted him; and he crowned it with a rakish optimism, as with the red cap of Liberty. He was in hearty sympathy with absolute Will; he praised it even for being vain and maleficent, if it was only proud enough to praise itself.

CHAPTER XI

NIETZSCHE AND SCHOPENHAUER

IT is hardly fair to a writer like Nietzsche, so poetical, fragmentary, and immature, to judge him as a philosopher; yet he wished to be so judged, and planned a system which was to be an emendation of that of Schopenhauer. The will to live would become the will to dominate; pessimism founded on reflection would become optimism founded on courage; the suspense of the will in contemplation would yield to a more biological account of intelligence and taste; finally in the place of pity and asceticism (Schopenhauer's two principles of morals) Nietzsche would set up the duty of asserting the will at all costs and being cruelly but beautifully strong.

These points of difference from Schopenhauer cover the whole philosophy of Nietzsche. I will consider them in order, leaving the last for the next chapter.

The change from 'the will to live' to 'the will to be powerful' is only a change of metaphors: both are used merely to indicate the general movement of nature. The choice of a psychological symbol for this purpose is indifferent scientifically, since the facts in any case

remain the same and our knowledge of them is not enlarged; yet it is an interesting indication of the mind of
the poet using it, because whatever a man knows and
loves best, that he takes his metaphors from. Nietzsche
had his reasons for liking to call the universal principle
a lust for power. He believed he was the herald of
two hundred years of war, he was in love with the vague
image of a military aristocracy, and he was not without
a certain biological acumen.

An acorn in the ground does not strive to persevere
in the state it happens to be in, but expands, absorbs
surrounding elements, and transforms them into its
own substance, which itself changes its form. Here
then is a will to grow, not simply a will to live or to
preserve oneself; in fact, as Nietzsche eloquently said,
here is a will to perish. It is true that when the oak is
full grown it seems to pass to the defensive and no longer
manifests the will either to perish or to grow. Even
while the will to grow is operating, its scope is not
indefinite. It would be grotesque to imagine that the
acorn, like the ego of German philosophy, tended to
annex the whole earth and the whole sky and to make a
single oak of the universe. If we take a broad view,
perhaps the ancient myth that nature tends to re-embody
certain fixed types, though inaccurate, gives a better
picture of the facts than the modern myth that she is
striving to change in one predetermined direction.
Nevertheless, the fact that Nietzsche's attention was

fascinated by the will to grow and to dominate shows that he was in sympathy with young things, that his heart was big with the future, and that his age believed in progress.

The change from pessimism to optimism, verbally so complete, did not imply any divergence between Nietzsche and Schopenhauer in their description of the facts; it was all a matter of a little more spirit in the younger thinker and a little more conscience in the elder. Romantic poets and their heroes are well known to oscillate between passionate despair and passionate enterprise. Schopenhauer affected passionate despair, Nietzsche recommended passionate enterprise, each being wedded exclusively to one of those moods which Faust or Byron could feel alternately and reduce to act with all the dashing tumult of anarchy. The value which the world has in the eyes of its inhabitants is necessarily mixed, so that a sweeping optimism or pessimism can be only a theoretic pose, false to the natural sentiment even of those who assume it. Both are impressionistic judgments passed on the world at large, not perhaps without some impertinence.

Yet it is these poses or attitudes, or, if you like, these impertinences, that give importance to transcendental philosophers; it is their representative and contagious side; their views of things would concern us little, if it were the things themselves that we wished to understand; but our whole study is a study in romanticism. The temper of the age ignored that man is a teachable animal living in a natural world. All that was a vulgar convention; in truth a disembodied Will was directed on any and every ideal at random, and when any of these fantastic objects seemed to be attained nothing was really accomplished, nothing was accumulated or learned. The wish for some other will-o'-the-wisp immediately succeeded, always equally passionate and equally foolish.

It is amazing that such a picture of human experience should have met with anything but general derision; but when people read books they compare them with other books, and when they turn to things they forget books altogether. Hence the most palpable falsehoods are held by general consent at certain moments, because they follow logically from what the books of the previous generation had maintained. This absurdity of Schopenhauer's is a plausible variation of idealism; to see how absurd it is you must remember the facts of life, the existence of any degree of civilization or progress. In these the travail of human nature appears; for human nature is not merely a name for a certain set of passions known to literature; in that sense Schopenhauer fully acknowledged it, and even thought it immutable; it is rather the constitution of an animal capable of training and development. What is more patent than that a man may learn something by experience and may be trained? But if he can be trained he is capable of adaptation and, therefore, of happiness, and the preposterous assertion

that all desires are equally arbitrary and equally fruitless
is blown to the winds.

The belief in a romantic chaos lends itself to pessimism
but it also lends itself to absolute self-assertion. Kant
had boasted that he had removed knowledge in order
to make room for faith; in other words, he had returned
to chaos in order to find freedom. The great egotists,
who detested the pressure of a world they had not
posited or created, followed gladly in that path; but
Schopenhauer was not an egotist. Like Goethe he was
probably more selfish personally than those other philosophers whom their very egotism had made zealous and
single-minded; but in imagination and feeling he was,
like Goethe, genial and humane: the freedom and ex-
uberance of nature impressed him more than his own.
Had he been an egotist, as Fichte, Hegel, and Nietzsche
were, he might have been an optimist like them. He
was rather a happy man, hugely enjoying a great many
things, among them food and music; and he taught that
music was a direct transcript of the tormented will to
live. How simple it would have been for him, if he
had been an egotist, to enjoy the spectacle of that
tormented will as much as the music which was its
faithful image! But no; such aesthetic cruelty, which
was Nietzsche's delight, would have revolted Schopenhauer. He thought tragedy beautiful because it de-
tached us from a troubled world and did not think a
troubled world good, as those unspeakable optimists did,

because it made such a fine tragedy. It is pleasant to find that among all these philosophers one at least was a gentleman.

If Will is the sole substance or force in the universe, it must be present in everything that exists, yet Schopenhauer affirmed that it was absent in aesthetic contemplation; and he looked to an ultimate denial of the will, which if it was to be an act and not merely a void would evidently be impossible on his principles. The Will might well say to those who attempted to deny it: 'They reckon ill who leave me out; when me they fly, I am the wings.' In perceiving and correcting this contradiction, Nietzsche certainly improved the technique of the system.

Yet that contradiction was not substantial; it was verbal merely, and due to the fond use of the term Will for what might more properly be called matter, energy, or movement. Will taken in the metaphorical sense can never be in abeyance, so long as anything is going on; but will taken in its proper sense is in abeyance often; and this is what Schopenhauer saw and meant to say. Actual and conscious will is a passing phenomenon; it is so little necessary to life that it always disappears when life is at its height. All pure pleasures, including those of seeing and thinking, are without it: they are ingenuous, and terminate in their present object. A philosopher should have learned from Aristotle, if not from his own experience, that at the acme of life we live in the eternal, and that then, as Schopenhauer said, we no longer pry but gaze, and are freed from willing.

This is not to say that Nietzsche was not very happy and witty in his description of the passions that dominate artists and philosophers, and in urging that the life of the spirit was an impassioned thing. To prove it, he might have quoted Schopenhauer himself, in those moving passages where he describes the ecstasy of thought and the spell of beauty. It is not the dead or the bloodless that have such feelings. Of course, if the operations of the brain, and the whole instinctive life of the soul, were interrupted neither these feelings nor any others would arise. This was at bottom Schopenhauer's conviction. His great intuition, the corner-stone of his philosophy, was precisely the priority of automatism and instinct over the intellect. His only error came from having given to these underlying processes the name of Will, when properly the will is one expression of them only, as the intellect is.

Nietzsche, who adopted the same metaphor, was led by it into the very confusion which he criticized in Schopenhauer. Nietzsche had no great technical competence: he saw the inconsistency only when he disliked the result; when the result fell in with his first impressions he repeated the inconsistency. He often condemned other moralists for being enemies to life: he reproached the greater part of mankind for loving inglorious ease and resenting the sufferings inseparable from the will to be mighty and to perish. But this churlish attitude of the vulgar would be quite impossible if the heroic will to be powerful were the essence of everybody and even of material things. If I am nothing but the will to grow, how can I ever will to shrink?

But this inconsistency in Nietzsche, like that in Schopenhauer, was an honourable one that came of forgetting a false generalization in the presence of a clear fact. That the will to be powerful is everywhere was a false generalization; but it was a clear fact that some people are pious Christians or Epicurean philosophers, who do not care at all about conquering the world. They want to be let alone, and perhaps have a shrewd suspicion that no one lives under such dire compulsions as he who undertakes to tyrannize over others. This slave-morality of theirs might be called will, though it is rather instinct and habit; but it is certainly not a will to be powerful: it is the opposite of that passion. Thus Nietzsche, by an honest self-contradiction, pointed to people who denied the will to be powerful, in order to abuse them, just as Schopenhauer had pointed to people who denied or suspended the will to live, in order to praise them.

CHAPTER XII

THE ETHICS OF NIETZSCHE

NIETZSCHE occasionally spoke disparagingly of morality, as if the word and the thing had got a little on his nerves; and some of his best-known phrases might give the impression that he wished to drop the distinction between good and evil and transcend ethics altogether. Such a thought would not have been absurd in itself or even unphilosophical. Many serious thinkers, Spinoza for instance, have believed that everything that happens is equally necessary and equally expressive of the will of God, be it favourable or unfavourable to our special interests and, therefore, called by us good or bad. A too reverent immersion in nature and history convinces them that to think any part of reality better or worse than the rest is impertinent or even impious. It is true that in the end these philosophers usually stultify themselves and declare enthusiastically that whatever is is right. This rapturous feeling can overcome anybody in certain moods, as it sometimes overcame Nietzsche; but in yielding to it, besides contradicting all other moral judgments, these mystics break their difficult resolution never to judge at all.

Nietzsche, however, was entirely free from this divine impediment in morals. The courage to cling to what his soul loved—and this courage is the essence of morality—was conspicuous in him. He was a poet, a critic, a lover of form and of distinctions. Few persons have ever given such fierce importance to their personal taste. What he disliked to think of, say democracy, he condemned with the fulminations of a god; what he liked to think of, power, he seriously commanded man and nature to pursue for their single object.

What Nietzsche disparaged, then, under the name of morality was not all morality, for he had an enthusiastic master-morality of his own to impose. He was thinking only of the Christian virtues and especially of a certain Protestant and Kantian moralism with which perhaps he had been surfeited. This moralism conceived that duty was something absolute and not a method of securing whatever goods of all sorts are attainable by action. The latter is the common and the sound opinion, maintained, for instance, by Aristotle; but Nietzsche, who was not humble enough to learn very much by study, thought he was propounding a revolutionary doctrine when he put goods and evils beyond and above right and wrong; for this is all that his *Jenseits von Gut und Böse* amounts to. Whatever seemed to him admirable, beautiful, eligible, whatever was good in the sense opposed not to *böse* but to *schlecht*,

Nietzsche loved with jealous affection. Hence his ire against Christianity, which he thought renounced too much. Hence his hatred of moralism, which in raising duty to the irresponsible throne of the absolute had superstitiously sacrificed half the goods of life. Nietzsche, then, far from transcending ethics, re-established it on its true foundations, which is not to say that the sketchy edifice which he planned to raise on these foundations was in a beautiful style of architecture or could stand at all.

The first principle of his ethics was that the good is power. But this word power seems to have had a great range of meanings in his mind. Sometimes it suggests animal strength and size, as in the big blond beast; sometimes vitality, sometimes fortitude, sometimes contempt for the will of others, sometimes (and this is perhaps the meaning he chiefly intended) dominion over natural forces and over the people, that is to say, wealth and military power. It is characteristic of this whole school that it confuses the laws which are supposed to preside over the movement of things with the good results which they may involve; so Nietzsche confuses his biological insight, that all life is the assertion of some sort of power—the power to breathe, for instance—with the admiration he felt for a masterful egotism. But even if we identify life or any kind of existence with the exertion of strength, the kinds of strength exerted will be heterogeneous and not always compatible.

The strength of Lucifer does not ensure victory in war; it points rather to failure in a world peopled by millions of timid, pious, and democratic persons. Hence we find Nietzsche asking himself plaintively, 'Why are the feeble victorious?' The fact rankled in his bosom that in the ancient world martial aristocracies had succumbed before Christianity, and in the modern world before democracy. By strength, then, he could not mean the power to survive, by being as flexible as circumstances may require. He did not refer to the strength of majorities, nor to the strength of vermin. At the same time he did not refer to moral strength, for of moral strength he had no idea.

The arts give power, but only in channels prescribed by their own principles, not by the will of untrained men. To be trained is to be tamed and harnessed, an accession of power detestable to Nietzsche. His Zarathustra had the power of dancing, also of charming serpents and eagles: no wonder that he missed the power, bestowed by goodness, of charming and guiding men; and a Terpsichorean autocrat would be hard to imagine. A man intent on algebra or on painting is not striving to rule anybody; his dominion over painting or algebra is chiefly a matter of concentration and self-forgetfulness. So dominion over the passions changes them from attempts to appropriate anything into sentiments of the mind, colouring a world which is no longer coveted. To attain such autumnal wisdom is, if you like, itself a power of feeling and a kind of strength; but it is not helpful in conquering the earth.

Nietzsche was personally more philosophical than his philosophy. His talk about power, harshness, and superb immorality was the hobby of a harmless young scholar and constitutional invalid. He did not crave in the least either wealth or empire. What he loved was solitude, nature, music, books. But his imagination, like his judgment, was captious; it could not dwell on reality, but reacted furiously against it. Accordingly, when he speaks of the will to be powerful, power is merely an eloquent word on his lips. It symbolizes the escape from mediocrity. What power would be when attained and exercised remains entirely beyond his horizon. What meets us everywhere is the sense of impotence and a passionate rebellion against it.

The phrases in which Nietzsche condensed and felt his thought were brilliant, but they were seldom just. We may perhaps see the principle of his ethics better if we forget for a moment the will to be powerful and consider this: that he knew no sort of good except the beautiful, and no sort of beauty except romantic stress. He was a belated prophet of romanticism. He wrote its epitaph, in which he praised it more extravagantly than anybody, when it was alive, had had the courage to do.

Consider, for example, what he said about truth. Since men were governed solely by the will to be powerful, the truth for its own sake must be moonshine to them. They would wish to cultivate such ideas, whether true or false, as might be useful to their ambition. Nietzsche (more candid in this than some other pragmatists) confessed that truth itself did not interest him; it was ugly; the bracing atmosphere of falsehood, passion, and subjective perspectives was the better thing. Sometimes, indeed, a more wistful mood overtook him, and he wondered whether the human mind would be able to endure the light of truth. That was the great question of the future. We may agree that a mind without poetry, fiction, and subjective colouring would not be human, nor a mind at all; and that neither truth nor the knowledge of truth would have any intrinsic value if nobody cared about it for its own sake. But some men do care; and in ignoring this fact Nietzsche expresses the false and pitiful notion that we can be interested in nothing except in ourselves and our own future. I am solitary, says the romantic egotist, and sufficient unto myself. The world is my idea, new every day: what can I have to do with truth?

This impulse to turn one's back on truth, whether in contempt or in despair, has a long history. Lessing had said that he preferred the pursuit of truth to the truth itself; but if we take this seriously (as possibly it was not meant) the pursuit of truth at once changes its character. It can no longer be the pursuit of truth, truth not being wanted, but only the pursuit of some

III

fresh idea. Whether one of these ideas or another comes nearer to the truth would be unimportant and undiscoverable. Any idea will do, so long as it is pregnant with another that may presently take its place; and as presumably error will precipitate new ideas more readily than truth, we might almost find it implied in Lessing's maxim that, as Nietzsche maintained, what is really good is neither truth nor the pursuit of truth (for you might find it, and what would you do then?), but rather a perpetual flux of errors.

This view is also implied in the very prevalent habit of regarding opinions as justified not by their object but by their date. The intellectual ignominy of believing what we believe simply because of the time and place of our birth, escapes many evolutionists. Far from trying to overcome this natural prejudice of position, they raise it into a point of pride. They declare all opinions ever held in the past to be superseded, and are apparently content that their own should be superseded to-morrow, but meantime they cover you with obloquy if you are so backward or so forward as not to agree with them to-day. They accept as inevitable the total dominion of the point of view. Each new date, even in the life of an individual thinker, is expected by them to mark a new phase of doctrine. Indeed, truth is an object which transcendental philosophy cannot envisage: the absolute ego must be satisfied with consistency. How should the truth, actual, natural, or divine, be an expression of the living will that attempts, or in their case despairs, to discover it? Yet that everything, even in truth, is an expression of the living will, is the corner-stone of this philosophy.

Consider further the spirit in which Nietzsche condemned Christianity and the Christian virtues. Many people have denounced Christianity on the ground that it was false or tyrannical, while perhaps admitting that it was comforting or had a good moral influence. Nietzsche denounced it—and in unmeasured terms—on the ground that (while, of course, as true as any other vital lie) it was mean, depressing, slavish, and plebeian. How beastly was the precept of love! Actually to love all these grotesque bipeds was degrading. A lover of the beautiful must wish almost all his neighbours out of the way. Compassion, too, was a lamentable way of assimilating oneself to evil. That contagious misery spoiled one's joy, freedom, and courage. Disease should not be nursed but cauterized; the world must be made clean.

Now there is a sort of love of mankind, a jealous love of what man might be, in this much decried maxim of unmercifulness. Nietzsche rebelled at the thought of endless wretchedness, pervasive mediocrity, crying children, domestic drudges, and pompous fools for ever. *Die Erde war zu lange schon ein Irrenhaus!* His heart was tender enough, but his imagination was impatient. When he praised cruelty, it was on the ground that art was cruel, that it made beauty out of suffering. Suffering, therefore, was good, and so was crime, which made life keener. Only crime, he said, raises a man high enough for the lightning to strike him. In the hope of sparing some obscure person a few groans or tears, would you deprive the romantic hero of so sublime a death?

Christians, too, might say they had their heroes, their saints; but what sort of eminence was that? It was produced by stifling half the passions. A sister of charity could not be an Arminius; devotion to such remedial offices spoilt the glory of life. Holiness was immoral; it was a half-suicide. *All* experience, the ideal of Faust, was what a spirited man must desire. All experience would involve, I suppose, passing through all the sensations of a murderer, a maniac, and a toad; even through those of a saint or a sister of charity. But the romantic mind despises results; it is satisfied with poses.

Consider, too, the romantic demand for a violent chiaroscuro, a demand which blossoms into a whole system of ethics. Good and evil, we are told, enhance one another, like light and shade in a picture; without evil there can be no good, to diminish the one is to undermine the other, and the greatest and most heroic man is he who not only does most good but also most harm. In his love of mischief, in his tenderness for the adventurer who boldly inflicts injury and suffering on others and on himself, in order to cut a more thrilling and stupendous figure in his own eyes, Nietzsche gave

this pernicious doctrine its frankest expression; but unfortunately it was not wholly his own. In its essence it
belongs to Hegel, and under various sophistical disguises
it has been adopted by all his academic followers in
England and America. The arguments used to defend
it are old sophisms borrowed from the Stoics, who
had turned the physical doctrine of Heraclitus, that
everything is a mixture of contraries, into an argument
for resignation to inevitable evils and detachment from
tainted goods. The Stoics, who were neither romantic
nor worldly, used these sophisms in an attempt to
extirpate the passions, not to justify them. They were
sufficiently refuted by the excellent Plutarch where he
observes that according to this logic it was requisite
and necessary that Thersites should be bald in order
that Achilles might have leonine hair. The absurdity
is, indeed, ludicrous, if we are thinking of real things
and of the goods and evils of experience; but egotists
never think of that; what they always think of is the
picture of those realities in their imagination. For the
observer, effects of contrast do alter the values of the
elements considered; and, indeed, the elements themselves, if one is very unsympathetic, may not have at all
in contemplation the quality they have in experience:
whence aesthetic cruelty. The respect which Hegel
and Nietzsche have for those sophisms becomes intelligible when we remember what imperturbable
egotists they were.

This egotism in morals is partly mystical. There is a luxurious joy in healing the smart of evil in one's mind, without needing to remove or diminish the evil in the world. The smart may be healed by nursing the conviction that evil after all is good, no matter how much of it there is or how much of it we do. In part, however, this egotism is romantic; it does not ask to be persuaded that evil, in the end, is good. It feels that evil is good in the present; it is so intense a thing to feel and so exciting a thing to do. Here we have what Nietzsche wished to bring about, a reversal of all values. To do evil is the true virtue, and to be good is the most hopeless vice. Milk is for babes; your strong man should be soaked in blood and in alcohol. We should live perilously; and as material life is the power to digest poisons, so true excellence is the power to commit all manner of crimes, and to survive.

That there is no God is proved by Nietzsche pragmatically, on the ground that belief in the existence of God would have made him uncomfortable. Not at all for the reason that might first occur to us: to imagine himself a lost soul has always been a point of pride with the romantic genius. The reason was that if there had been any gods he would have found it intolerable not to be a god himself. Poor Nietzsche! The laurels of the Almighty would not let him sleep.

It is hard to know if we should be more deceived in taking these sallies seriously or in not taking them so. On the one hand it all seems the swagger of an immature, half-playful mind, like a child that tells you he will cut your head off. The dreamy impulse, in its inception, is sincere enough, but there is no vestige of any understanding of what it proposes, of its conditions, or of its results. On the other hand these explosions are symptomatic; there stirs behind them unmistakably an elemental force. That an attitude is foolish, incoherent, disastrous, proves nothing against the depth of the instinct that inspires it. Who could be more intensely unintelligent than Luther or Rousseau? Yet the world followed them, not to turn back. The molecular forces of society, so to speak, had already undermined the systems which these men denounced. If the systems have survived it is only because the reformers, in their intellectual helplessness, could supply nothing to take their place. So Nietzsche, in his genial imbecility, betrays the shifting of great subterranean forces. What he said may be nothing, but the fact that he said it is all-important. Out of such wild intuitions, because the heart of the child was in them, the man of the future may have to build his philosophy. We should forgive Nietzsche his boyish blasphemies. He hated with clearness, if he did not know what to love.

CHAPTER XIII

THE SUPERMAN

In his views on matters of fact Nietzsche, as becomes the naïve egotist, was quite irresponsible. If he said the course of history repeated itself in cycles, it was because the idea pleased him; it seemed a symbol of self-approval on the world's part. If he hailed the advent of a race of men superior to ourselves and of stronger fibre, it was because human life as it is, and especially his own life, repelled him. He was sensitive and, therefore, censorious. He gazed about him, he gazed at himself, he remembered the disappointing frailties and pomposity of the great man, Wagner, whom he had once idolized. His optimism for the moment yielded to his sincerity. He would sooner abolish than condone such a world, and he fled to some solitary hillside by the sea, saying to himself that man was a creature to be superseded.

Dissatisfaction with the actual is what usually leads people to frame ideals at all, or at least to hold them fast; but such a negative motive leaves the ideal vague and without consistency. If we could suddenly have our will, we should very likely find the result trivial or horrible. So the superman of Nietzsche might prove, if by magic he could be realized. To frame solid ideals, which would, in fact, be better than actual things, is not granted to the merely irritable poet; it is granted only to the master-workman, to the modeller of some given substance to some given use—things which define his aspiration, and separate what is relevant and glorious in his dreams from that large part of them which is merely ignorant and peevish. It was not for Nietzsche to be an artist in morals and to institute anything coherent, even in idea.

The superman of Nietzsche is rendered the more chimerical by the fact that he must contradict not only the common man of the present but also the superior men, the half-superhuman men, of the past. To transcend humanity is no new ambition; that has always been the effort of Indian and Christian religious discipline and of Stoic philosophy. But this spiritual superiority, like that of artists and poets, has come of abstraction; a superiority to life, in that these minds were engrossed in the picture or lesson of life rather than in living; and if they powerfully affected the world, as they sometimes did, it was by bringing down into it something supermundane, the arresting touch of an ulterior wisdom. Nietzsche, on the contrary, even more than most modern philosophers, loved mere life with the pathetic intensity of the wounded beast; his superman must not rise above our common condition by his purely spiritual resources, or by laying up his treasure in any sort of heaven. He must be not a superior man but a kind of physiological superman, a griffin in soul, if not in body, who instead of labouring hands and religious faith should have eagle's wings and the claws of a lion. His powers should be superior to ours by resembling those of fiercer and wilder animals. The things that make a man tame—Nietzsche was a retired professor living in a boarding-house—must be changed into their opposites. But man has been tamed by agriculture, material arts, children, experience; therefore these things are to be far from the superman. If he must resemble somebody, it will be rather the *condottieri* of the Renaissance or the princes and courtiers of the seventeenth century; Caesar Borgia is the supreme instance. He must have a splendid presence and address, gallantry, contempt for convention, loyalty to no country, no woman, and no idea, but always a buoyant and lordly assertion of instinct and of self. In the helter-skelter of his irritable genius, Nietzsche jumbled together the ferocity of solitary beasts, the indifference and *hauteur* of patricians, and the antics of revellers, and out of that mixture he hoped to evoke the rulers of the coming age.

How could so fantastic an ideal impose on a keen satirist like Nietzsche and a sincere lover of excellence? Because true human excellence seemed to him hostile to life, and he felt—this was his strong and sane side, his lien on the future—that life must be accepted as it is or may become, and false beliefs, hollow demands, and hypocritical, forced virtues must be abandoned. This new wisdom was that which Goethe, too, had felt and practised; and of all masters of life Goethe was the one whom Nietzsche could best understand. But a master of life, without being in the least hostile to life, since he fulfils it, nevertheless uses life for ends which transcend it. Even Goethe, omnivorous and bland as he was, transcended life in depicting and judging and blessing it. The saints and the true philosophers have naturally emphasized more this renunciation of egotism: they have seen all things in the light of eternity—that is, as they are in truth—and have consequently felt a reasonable contempt for mere living and mere dying; and in that precisely lies moral greatness. Here Nietzsche could not follow: rationality chilled him; he craved vehemence.

How life can be fulfilled and made beautiful by reason was never better shown than by the Greeks, both by precept and example. Nietzsche in his youth was a professor of Greek literature: one would have expected his superman to be a sort of Greek hero. Something of the Dorian harshness in beauty, something of the Pindaric high-born and silent victor, may have been fused into Nietzsche's ideal; certainly Bacchic freedom and ardour were to enter in. But on the whole it is remarkable how little he learned from the

Greeks, no modesty or reverence, no joy in order and in loveliness, no sense for friendship, none for the sanctity of places and institutions. He repeated the paradoxes of some of their sophists, without remembering how their wise men had refuted them. For example, he gave a new name and a new prominence to the distinction between what he called the Dionysiac and the Apollonian elements in Greek genius. He saw how false was that white-washed notion of the Greek mind which young ladies derived from sketching a plaster cast of the Apollo Belvedere.[1] He saw that a demonic force, as the generation of Goethe called it, underlay everything; what he did not see was that this demonic force was under control, which is the secret of the whole matter. The point had been thoroughly elucidated by Plato, in the contrast he drew between inspiration and art. But Plato was rather ironical about inspiration, and had a high opinion of art; and Nietzsche, with his contrary instinct, rushes away without understanding the mind of the master or the truth of the situation. He thinks he alone has discovered the divinity of Dionysus and of the Muses, which Plato took as a matter of course

[1] I was about to say, how false was the notion of Winkelmann about the grandeur and repose of the Greek spirit. But Winkelmann, if his sense for the chained monsters in the Greek soul was inadequate, was at least in real sympathy with what had inspired Greek sculpture, love and knowledge of the human body in the life, made gentle by discipline and kept strong by training. For that reason Winkelmann seems hardly a German: his learning was deficient and his heart was humble. He did not patronize the ancients, he believed in them.

but would not venerate superstitiously. Inspiration, like will, is a force without which reason can do nothing. Inspiration must be presupposed; but in itself it can do nothing good unless it is in harmony with reason, or is brought into harmony with it. This two-edged wisdom that makes impulse the stuff of life and reason its criterion, is, of course, lost on Nietzsche, and with it the whole marvel of Greek genius. There is nothing exceptional in being alive and impulsive; any savage can run wild and be frenzied and enact histrionic passions: the virtue of the Greeks lay in the exquisite firmness with which they banked their fires without extinguishing them, so that their life remained human (indeed, remained infra-human, like that of Nietzsche's superman) and yet became beautiful: they were severe and fond of maxims, on a basis of universal tolerance; they governed themselves rationally, with a careful freedom, while well aware that nature and their own bosoms were full of gods, all of whom must be reverenced.

After all, this defect in appreciation is inseparable from the transcendental pose. The ancients, like everything else, never seem to the egotist a reality co-ordinate with himself, from which he might still have something to learn. They are only so much 'content' for his self-consciousness, so much matter for his thought to transcend. They can contain nothing for him but the part of his outgrown self which he deigns to identify with them. His mind must always envelop them and be the larger thing. No wonder that in this school learning is wasted for the purposes of moral education. Whoever has seen the learned egotist flies at his approach. History in his hands is a demonstration of his philosophy. Science is a quarry of proofs for his hobbies. If we do not agree with him we are not merely mistaken (every philosopher tells us that), but we are false to ourselves and ignorant of our ideal significance. His ego gives us our place in the world. He informs us of what we mean, whatever we may say; and he raises our opinions, as he might his food, to a higher unity in his own person. He is priest in every temple. He approaches a picture-gallery or a foreign religion in a dictatorial spirit, with his *a priori* categories ready on his lips; pedantry and vanity speak in his every gesture, and the lesson of nothing can reach his heart.

No, neither the philosophy inherited by Nietzsche nor his wayward imagination was fit to suggest to him a nobler race of men. On the contrary, they shut him off from comprehension of the best men that have existed. Like the Utopias or ideals of many other satirists and minor philosophers, the superman is not a possibility, it is only a protest. Our society is outworn, but hard to renew; the emancipated individual needs to master himself. In what spirit or to what end he will do so, we do not know, and Nietzsche cannot tell us. He is the jester, to whom all incoherences are forgiven, because all indiscretions are allowed. His mind is undisciplined, and his tongue outrageous, but he is at bottom the friend of our conscience, and full of shrewd wit and tender wisps of intuition. Behind his 'gay wisdom' and trivial rhymes lies a great anguish. His intellect is lost in a chaos. His heart denies itself the relief of tears and can vent itself only in forced laughter and mock hopes that gladden nobody, least of all himself.

CHAPTER XIV

HEATHENISM

SCHOPENHAUER somewhere observes that the word heathen, no longer in reputable use elsewhere, had found a last asylum in Oxford, the paradise of dead philosophies. Even Oxford, I believe, has now abandoned it; yet it is a good word. It conveys, as no other word can, the sense of vast multitudes tossing in darkness, harassed by demons of their own choice. No doubt it implies also a certain sanctimony in the superior person who uses it, as if he at least were not chattering in the general babel. What justified Jews, Christians, and Moslems (as Mohammed in particular insisted) in feeling this superiority was the possession of a book, a chart of life, as it were, in which the most important features of history and morals were mapped out for the guidance of teachable men. The heathen, on the contrary, were abandoned to their own devices, and even prided themselves on following only their spontaneous will, their habit, presumption, or caprice.

Most unprejudiced people would now agree that the value of those sacred histories and rules of life did not depend on their alleged miraculous origin, but rather on that solidity and perspicacity in their authors which enabled them to perceive the laws of sweet and profitable conduct in this world. It was not religion merely that was concerned, at least not that outlying, private, and almost negligible sphere to which we often apply this name; it was the whole fund of experience mankind had gathered by living; it was wisdom. Now, to record these lessons of experience, the Greeks and Romans also had their books; their history, poetry, science, and civil law. So that while the theologically heathen may be those who have no Bible, the morally and essentially heathen are those who possess no authoritative wisdom, or reject the authority of what wisdom they have; the untaught or unteachable who disdain not only revelation but what revelation stood for among early peoples, namely, funded experience.

In this sense the Greeks were the least heathen of men. They were singularly docile to political experiment, to law, to methodical art, to the proved limitations and resources of mortal life. This life they found closely hedged about by sky, earth, and sea, by war, madness, and conscience with their indwelling deities, by oracles and local genii with their accustomed cults, by a pervasive fate, and the jealousy of invisible gods. Yet they saw that these divine forces were constant, and that they exercised their pressure and bounty with so much method that a prudent art and religion could be built up in their midst. All this was simply a poetic prologue to science and the arts; it largely passed into them, and would have passed into them altogether if the naturalistic genius of Greece had not been crossed in Socrates by a premature discouragement, and diverted into other channels.

Early Hebraism itself had hardly been so wise. It had regarded its tribal and moral interests as absolute, and the Creator as the champion and omnipotent agent of Israel. But this arrogance and inexperience were heathen. Soon the ascendency of Israel over nature and history was proclaimed to be conditional on their fidelity to the Law; and as the spirit of the nation under chastisement became more and more penitential, it was absorbed increasingly in the praise of wisdom. Salvation was to come only by repentance, by being born again with a will wholly transformed and broken; so that the later Jewish religion went almost as far as Platonism or Christianity in the direction opposite to heathenism.

This movement in the direction of an orthodox wisdom was regarded as a progress in those latter days of antiquity when it occurred, and it continued to be so regarded in Christendom until the rise of romanticism. The most radical reformers simply urged that the current orthodoxy, religious or scientific, was itself imperfectly orthodox, being corrupt, overloaded, too vague, or too narrow. As every actual orthodoxy is

avowedly incomplete and partly ambiguous, a sympathetic reform of it is always in order. Yet very often
the reformers are deceived. What really offends them
may not be what is false in the received orthodoxy, but
what though true is uncongenial to them. In that case
heathenism, under the guise of a search for a purer
wisdom, is working in their souls against wisdom of
any sort. Such is the suspicion that Catholics would
throw on Protestantism, naturalists on idealism, and
conservatives generally on all revolutions.

But if ever heathenism needed to pose as constructive
reform, it is now quite willing and able to throw off the
mask. Desire for any orthodox wisdom at all may be
repudiated; it may be set down to low vitality and
failure of nerve. In various directions at once we see
to-day an intense hatred and disbelief gathering head
against the very notion of a cosmos to be discovered,
or a stable human nature to be respected. Nature, we
are told, is an artificial symbol employed by life; truth
is a temporary convention; art is an expression of
personality; war is better than peace, effort than achievement, and feeling than intelligence; change is deeper
than form; will is above morality. Expressions of this
kind are sometimes wanton and only half thought out;
but they go very deep in the subjective direction.
Behind them all is a sincere revulsion against the
difficult and confused undertakings of reason; against
science, institutions, and moral compulsions. They

K   129

mark an honest retreat into immediate experience and animal faith. Man used to be called a rational animal, but his rationality is something eventual and ideal, whereas his animality is actual and profound. Heathenism, if we consider life at large, is the primal and universal religion.

It has never been my good fortune to see wild beasts in the jungle, but I have sometimes watched a wild bull in the ring, and I can imagine no more striking, simple, and heroic example of animal faith; especially when the bull is what is technically called noble, that is, when he follows the lure again and again with eternal single-ness of thought, eternal courage, and no suspicion of a hidden agency that is mocking him. What the red rag is to this brave creature, their passions, inclinations, and chance notions are to the heathen. What they will they will; and they would deem it weakness and dis-loyalty to ask whether it is worth willing or whether it is attainable. The bull, magnificently sniffing the air, surveys the arena with the cool contempt and disbelief of the idealist, as if he said: 'You seem, you are a seeming; I do not quarrel with you, I do not fear you. I am real, you are nothing.' Then suddenly, when his eye is caught by some bright cloak displayed before him, his whole soul changes. His will awakes and he seems to say: 'You are my destiny; I want you, I hate you, you shall be mine, you shall not stand in my path. I will gore you. I will disprove you. I will

pass beyond you. I shall be, you shall not have been.'
Later, when sorely wounded and near his end, he grows
blind to all these excitements. He smells the moist
earth, and turns to the dungeon where an hour ago he
was at peace. He remembers the herd, the pasture
beyond, and he dreams: 'I shall not die, for I love life.
I shall be young again, young always, for I love youth.
All this outcry is naught to me, this strange suffering
is naught. I will go to the fields again, to graze, to
roam, to love.'

So exactly, with not one least concession to the
unsuspected reality, the heathen soul stands bravely
before a painted world, covets some bauble, and defies
death. Heathenism is the religion of will, the faith
which life has in itself because it is life, and in its aims
because it is pursuing them.

In their tentative, many-sided, indomitable way,
the Germans have been groping for four hundred
years towards a restoration of their primitive heathenism.
Germany under the long tutelage of Rome had been
like a spirited and poetic child brought up by very old
and very worldly foster-parents. For many years the
elfin creature may drink in their gossip and their maxims
with simple wonder; but at last he will begin to be
restive under them, ask himself ominous questions,
protest, suffer, and finally break into open rebellion.
Naturally he will not find at first theories and precepts
of his own to take the place of his whole education; he

will do what he can with his traditions, revising, interpreting, and patching them with new ideas; and only if
he has great earnestness and speculative power will he
ever reach an unalloyed expression of his oppressed
soul.

Now in Germany speculative power and earnestness existed in a high degree, not, of course, in most
people, but in the best and most representative; and
it was this *élite* that made the Reformation, and carried
it on into historical criticism and transcendental philosophy, until in the nineteenth century, in Schopenhauer,
Wagner, and Nietzsche, the last remnants of Christian
education were discarded and the spontaneous heathen
morality of the race reasserted itself in its purity.   That
this assertion was not consistent, that it was thrown into
the language and images of some alien system, is not to be
wondered at; but the Christianity of Parsifal, like the
Buddhism of the denial of the will, is a pure piece of
romanticism, an exotic setting for those vacillations and
sinkings which absolute Will may very well be subject
to in its absolute chaos.

The rebellion of the heathen soul is unmistakable
in the Reformation, but it is not recognized in this
simple form, because those who feel that it was justified
do not dream that it was heathen, and those who see
that it was heathen will not admit that it was justified.
Externally, of course, it was an effort to recover the
original essence of Christianity; but why should a free

and absolute being care for that original essence when he has discovered it, unless his own mind demanded that very thing? And if his mind demanded it, what need has he to read that demand into an ancient revelation which, as a matter of fact, turned on quite other matters? It was simply the inertia of established prejudice that made people use tradition to correct tradition; until the whole substance of tradition, worn away by that internal friction, should be dissolved, and impulse and native genius should assert themselves unimpeded.

Judaism and Christianity, like Greek philosophy, were singly inspired by the pursuit of happiness, in whatever form it might be really attainable: now on earth if possible, or in the millennium, or in some abstracted and inward life, like that of the Stoics, or, in the last resort, in a different life altogether beyond the grave. But heathenism ignores happiness, despises it, or thinks it impossible. The regimen and philosophy of Germany are inspired by this contempt for happiness, for one's own happiness as well as for other people's. Happiness seems to the German moralists something unheroic, an abdication before external things, a victory of the senses over the will. They think the pursuit of happiness low, materialistic, and selfish. They wish everybody to sacrifice or rather to forget happiness, and to do 'deeds.'

It is in the nature of things that those who are incapable of happiness should have no idea of it.

Happiness is not for wild animals, who can only oscillate between apathy and passion. To be happy, even to conceive happiness, you must be reasonable or (if Nietzsche prefers the word) you must be tamed. You must have taken the measure of your powers, tasted the fruits of your passions and learned your place in the world and what things in it can really serve you. To be happy you must be wise. This happiness is sometimes found instinctively, and then the rudest fanatic can hardly fail to see how lovely it is; but sometimes it comes of having learned something by experience (which empirical people never do) and involves some chastening and renunciation; but it is not less sweet for having this touch of holiness about it, and the spirit of it is healthy and beneficent. The nature of happiness, therefore, dawns upon philosophers when their wisdom begins to report the lessons of experience: an *a priori* philosophy can have no inkling of it.

Happiness is the union of vitality with art, and in so far as vitality is a spiritual thing and not mere restlessness and vehemence, art increases vitality. It obviates friction, waste, and despair. Without art, vitality is painful and big with monsters. It is hurried easily into folly and crime; it ignores the external forces and interests which it touches. German philosophy does this theoretically, by dethroning the natural world and calling it an idea created by the ego for its own purposes; and it does this practically also by obeying the categorical imperative—no longer the fabled imperatives of Sinai or of Königsberg, but the inward and vital imperative which the bull obeys, when trusting absolutely in his own strength, rage, and courage, he follows a little red rag and his destiny this way and that way.

CHAPTER XV

IT is customary to judge religions and philosophies by their truth, which is seldom their strong point; yet the application of that unsympathetic criterion is not unjust, since they aspire to be true, maintain that they are so, and forbid any opposed view, no matter how obvious and inevitable, to be called true in their stead. But when religions and philosophies are dead, or when we are so removed from them by time or training that the question of their truth is not a living question for us, they do not on that account lose all their interest; then, in fact, for the first time they manifest their virtues to the unbeliever. He sees that they are expressions of human genius; that however false to their subject-matter they may be, like the conventions of art they are true to the eye and to the spirit that fashioned them. And as nothing in the world, not even the truth, is so interesting as human genius, these incredible or obsolete religions and philosophies become delightful to us. The sting is gone out of their errors, which no longer threaten to delude us, and they have acquired a beauty invisible to the eye of their authors, because of the very refraction which the truth suffered in that vital medium.

136

German philosophy is a work of genius. To be heathen is easy; to have an absolute will and a belief in chaos—or rather a blind battle with chance—is probably the lot of most animals; but to be condemned to be learned, industrious, moral, and Christian, and yet, through that veil of unavoidable phenomena and conventions, to pierce to absolute will and freedom, and to set them forth persuasively as the true reality, in spite of all the ordered appearances which do not cease to confront and to occupy us—that is a work of genius. It is a wonderful achievement, to have recovered atavistically the depths of the primitive soul, in the midst of its later sophistication. In this philosophy the ancestral ego, the soul perplexed and incredulous at being born into this world, returns to haunt us in broad daylight and to persuade us with its ghostly eloquence that not that ego but this world is the ghost.

The egotism which in German philosophy is justified by a theory, in German genius is a form of experience. It turns everything it touches into a part of its own life, personal, spontaneous, sincere, original. It is young and self-sufficient; yet as a continual change of view is incompatible with art and learning, we see in Germany, even more than elsewhere, a division of labour between genius and tradition; nowhere are the types of the young rebel and the tireless pedant so common and so extreme.

The notion that something that moves and lives, as genius does, can at the same time be absolute has

some interesting implications. Such a genius and all
its works must be unstable. As it has no external
sources and no external objects, as its own past can
exercise no control over it (for that would be the most
lifeless of tyrannies), it is a sort of shooting star, with
no guarantees for the future. This, for the complete
egotist, has no terrors. A tragic end and a multitude
of enemies may seem good to the absolute hero and
necessary to his perfect heroism. In the same way, to
be without a subject-matter or an audience may seem
good to the absolute poet, who sings to himself as he
goes, exclusively for the benefit of that glorious and
fleeting moment. Genius could not be purer than that:
although perhaps it might be hard to prove that it was
genius.

A kindred implication, which perhaps might be
less welcome to the egotist himself, is that an absolute genius is formless, and that the absolute freedom
with which it thinks it takes on now this form and
now that, is not really freedom at all, but subjection
to unknown and perhaps ironical forces. Absolute
Will, of which a perfectly free genius is an expression,
cannot say specifically what it craves, for essentially
it should crave everything indiscriminately. In practice,
however, it must seem to aim at this or that precise
result. These specific aims are suggested to it by
circumstances, foisted upon it in its replete innocence;
for it is all expectation, all vague heartiness and zeal for

it knows not what. The logic it proclaims at any time and calls eternal is but the fashionable rhetoric of that hour. Absolute Will is a great dupe on whom fortune forces card after card. Like Faust it is helpless before the most vulgar temptations. Why should it not fulfil itself now by the pursuit of magic, now by the seduction of a young girl, now by an archaeological pose, now by a piratical or an engineering enterprise? True, there are limits to its gullibility; there are suggestions from which it recoils. The German ego, after swallowing Christianity whole, will in Luther stick at Indulgences. Faust sometimes turns on Mephistopheles, as the worm will turn: he says that he covets all experience, but in that he does himself a great injustice; there are experiences he scorns. After all this ego is not really absolute; it is specifically and pathetically human and directed upon a few natural ends. That is what saves it; for a mind can have no distinction and a soul no honour if its only maxim is to live on. It may take up with enthusiasm whatever it takes up, but it will take up anything; and it may do mightily whatever it does, but it will not do it long.

Consider, in this respect, the pathetic history of the German people. It conquered the Roman empire and it became Roman, or wished to become so. It had had a mythology and a morality of its own (very like in principle to those it has since rediscovered), yet it accepted Christianity with the docility of a child.

It began to feel, after some centuries, how alien to its genius this religion was, but it could find relief only in a fresh draught from the same foreign sources, or others more remote. To cease to be Roman it tried to become Hebraic and Greek. In studying these models, however it came upon a new scent. What passed for revelation or for classical perfection was of human national growth, stratified like the rocks, and not divine or authoritative at all. If you only made hypotheses enough, you could prove how it all arose according to necessary laws, logical, psychological, historical, economical, and aesthetical. Above all, you could prove how nobody had understood anything properly before, and how the key to it all was in your single hand.

Yet the triumphs of theory alone soon seemed unsatisfying. Wine, science, and song once seemed to make Germany happy, but if a prince imposed military discipline, might not that be an even better thing? For a time wistfulness, longing, and the feeling of Titanic loneliness and of a world to be evoked and snuffed out like a dream, seemed to fill the cup of intense living, and the greatest and happiest of Germans could cry:

> Nur wer die Sehnsucht kennt
> weiss, was ich leide,
> allein und abgetrennt
> von aller Freude.

But presently true intensity of life appeared to lie rather in being a victorious general, or an ironmaster, or a commercial traveller, or a reveller in the Friedrich-strasse, or a spy and conspirator anywhere in the world.

All these turbid and nondescript ambitions are in a sense artificial; the Germans accept them now as a thousand years ago they accepted Christianity, because such things are suddenly thrust upon them. By nature they are simple, honest, kindly, easily pleased. There is no latent irony or disbelief in their souls. The pleasures of sense, plain and copious, they enjoy hugely, long labour does not exasperate them, science fills them with satisfaction, music entrances them. There ought to be no happier or more innocent nation in this world. Unfortunately their very goodness and simplicity render them helpless; they are what they are dragooned to be. There is no social or intellectual disease to which, in spots, they do not succumb, as to an epidemic: their philosophy itself is an example of this. They have the defects of the newly prosperous; they are far too proud of their possessions, esteeming them for being theirs, without knowing whether they are good of their kind. Culture is a thing seldom mentioned by those who have it. The real strength of the Germans lies not in those external achievements of which at this moment they make so much—for they may outgrow this new material-ism of theirs—it lies rather in what they have always prized, their *Gemüth* and their music.

Perhaps these two things have a common root. Emotion is inarticulate, yet there is a mighty movement in it, and a great complexity of transitions and shades. This intrinsic movement of the feelings is ordinarily little noticed because people are too wide awake, or too imaginative. Everything is a fact or a picture to them, and their emotions seem to them little but obvious qualities of things. They roundly call *things* beautiful, painful, holy, or ridiculous; they do not speak of their *Gemüth*, although, of course, it is by virtue of their emotions that they pass such judgments. But when the occasions of our emotions, the objects that call them forth, are not so instantly focused, when we know better what we feel than why we feel it, then we seem to have a richer and more massive sensibility. Our feelings absorb our attention because they remain a thing apart: they seem to us wonderfully deep because we do not ground them in things external.

Now music is a means of giving form to our inner feelings without attaching them to events or objects in the world. Music is articulate, but articulate in a language which avoids, or at least veils, the articulation of the world we live in; it is, therefore, the chosen art of a mind to whom the world is still foreign. If this seems in one way an incapacity, it is also a privilege. Not to be at home in the world, to prize it chiefly for echoes which it may have in the soul, to have a soul that can give forth echoes, or that can generate internal dramas of sound out of its own resources—may this not be a more enviable endowment than that of a mind all surface, a sensitive plate only able to photograph this not too beautiful earth? In any case, for better or for worse, inward sensibility, unabsorbed in worldly affairs, exists in some people; a life, as it were, still in the womb and not yet in contact with the air. But let these inspired musicians, masters in their own infinite realms, beware of the touch of matter. Let them not compose a system of the universe out of their *Gemüth*, as they might a symphony. Let them not raise their baton in the face of the stars or of the nations, and think to lead them like an orchestra.

CHAPTER XVI

EGOTISM IN PRACTICE

THEORIES in their own ethereal essence can have no influence on events. But the men who conceive and adopt a theory, form, in doing so, certain habits of discrimination and of reaction to things. In fact, they have conceived and adopted their theory because their habits of apprehension and action suggested it to them, or could be brought to suggest it: the explicit theory is a symbol and omen of their practical attitude, of their way, as the phrase has it, of grasping the situation.

All philosophies have the common property of being speculative, and, therefore, their immediate influence on those who hold them is in many ways alike, however opposed the theories may be to one another: they all make people theoretical. In this sense any philosophy, if warmly embraced, has a moralizing force, because, even if it belittles morality, it absorbs the mind in intellectual contemplation, accustoms it to wide and reasoned comparisons, and makes the sorry escapades of human nature from convention seem even more ignominious than its ruling prejudices.

The particular theory of egotism arises from an

exorbitant interest in ourselves, in the medium of thought and action rather than in its objects. It is not necessarily incorrect, because the self is actual and indispensable; but the insistence on it is a little abnormal, because the self, like consciousness, ought to be diaphanous. Egotism in philosophy is, therefore, a probable symptom of excessive pedantry and inordinate self-assertion.

In the lofty theory of egotism life is represented as a sort of game of patience, in which the rules, the cards, the table, and the empty time on our hands, all are mere images created by the fancy, as in a dream. The *sense* of being occupied, though one really has nothing to do, will then be the secret of the whole affair, and the sole good to be attained by living. Of course this fantastic theory is put forward only on great occasions, when an extreme profundity is in place; but like other esoteric doctrines it expresses very well the spirit in which those people live habitually who would appeal to it in the last resort. Obviously such an egotist should in consistency be a man of principle. He would feel it to be derogatory to his dignity, and contrary to his settled purpose, to cheat at the game he has instituted. That luck should sometimes go against him is pre-ordained by himself; otherwise the game would have no zest, and to be interested, to be pressed, even to be annoyed seems the highest good to him in his great tedium. He will, therefore, be assiduous, patient, and law-abiding; and the idea of ever abandoning his chosen game for anything less forced and less arbitrary will seem to him disloyalty to himself, and a great wickedness.

Indeed, nothing beside his own purpose will have any value in his eyes, or even any existence. He will therefore inevitably act without consideration for others, without courtesy, without understanding. When he chooses to observe anything external—and he is studious —his very attentions will be an insult; for he will assume that his idea of that external thing is the reality of it, and that other people can have only such rights and only such a character as he is willing to assign to them. It follows from his egotistical principles that in judging others he should be officious and rude, learned and mistaken.

What the egotist calls his will and his ideals are, taken together, simply his passions; but the passions of the egotist are turned into a system and go unrebuked. A man who lowers his precepts to the level of his will may the more easily raise his practice to the level of his precepts. He endows his life with a certain coherence, momentum, and integrity, just because he has suppressed all vain aspiration and all useless shame. He does not call himself a sinner; he would be at a loss for a reason to think himself one; for really his standard of virtue expresses nothing but his prevalent will. Is it not intelligible that such a morality should be more efficacious, more unifying, heavier, and more convinced than one which begins by condemning our natural passions and the habitual course of human life?

In fact, egotism in practice is a solemn and arduous business; there is nothing malicious about it and nothing gay. There is rather a stolid surprise that such honest sentiments and so much enterprise should not meet everywhere with applause. If other people are put thereby at a disadvantage, why should they not learn their lesson and adopt in their turn the methods of the superman? If they are touched by the vanity and the charm of existence and neglect the intense pursuit of their absolute will, why do they complain if they are jostled and beaten? Only he deserves life and freedom, said Goethe, who is forced daily to win them afresh.

If the egotist suffers passion to speak in his philosophy, it is perhaps because he has so little passion. Men of frank passions quickly see the folly of them; but the passions of the egotist are muffled, dull, like the miserly passions of old men; they are diffused into sensuality and sentiment, or hardened into maxims. Egotistical lovers can hold hands for hours and chastely kiss each other for years; such tokens of affection help to keep them in love and at the same time are a sop to more troublesome impulses. Sentimentality and gush mark the absence of passion: the blood has been diluted to lymph. Hence the egotist can the more easily mistake his passions for duties, and his cupidities for ideals.

His devotion to these ideals is pure and enthusiastic; but in serving them he fattens steadily, as punctual at his work as at his meals, as dutifully moved by the approved music as by the official patriotism, vicious when it seems manly to be vicious, brutal when it seems politic to be brutal; he feels he is impeccable, and he must die in his sins. Nothing can ruffle the autonomous conscience of this kind of idealist, whose nature may be gross, but whose life is busy and conventional, and who loudly congratulates himself daily on all he knows and does.

Turn the circumstances about as you like, the egotist finds only one ultimate reason for everything. It is not a reason; it is absolute will. Suppose we asked the ego, in the Fichtean system, why it posited a material world to be its implacable enemy and rebellious toy, and why without necessity it raised this infinity of trouble for itself and for the unhappy world which it created by its fiat. It could only reply: 'Because such is the categorical imperative within me; because so I will, so I must, and so my absolute duty and its logic require. If the consequences are tragic—and in the end I know they must be tragic—that only proves the sublime unselfishness of my egotism, the purity of my sacred folly, the ideality of my groundless will. All reasons, all justifications which might appeal to me must be posterior to my will; my will itself can have no justification and no reason.'

Let us admire the sincerity of this searching confession. Virtue itself, if it relied on self-consciousness for its philosophy, could not justify itself on other grounds. If the difference between virtue and vice is hereby obliterated, that only proves that the difference is not founded on self-consciousness but on the circumstances and powers under which we live. What self-consciousness can disclose is not the basis of anything. All will is the expression of some animal body, frail and mortal, but teachable and rich in resource. The environment in which this will finds itself controls and rewards its various movements, and establishes within it the difference between virtue and vice, wisdom and folly.

The whole transcendental philosophy, if made ultimate, is false, and nothing but a private perspective. The will is absolute neither in the individual nor in humanity. Nature is not a product of the mind, but on the contrary there is an external world, ages prior to any idea of it, which the mind recognizes and feeds upon. There is a steady human nature within us, which our moods and passions may wrong but cannot annul. There is no categorical imperative but only the operation of instincts and interests more or less subject to discipline and mutual adjustment. Our whole life is a compromise, an incipient loose harmony between the passions of the soul and the forces of nature, forces which likewise generate and protect the souls of other creatures, endowing them with powers of expression and self-assertion comparable with our own, and with aims no less sweet and worthy in their own eyes; so that the quick and honest mind cannot but practise courtesy in the universe, exercising its will without vehemence or forced assurance, judging with serenity, and in everything discarding the word absolute as the most false and the most odious of words. As Montaigne observes, 'He who sets before him, as in a picture, this vast image of our mother Nature in her entire majesty; who reads in her aspect such universal and continual variety; who discerns himself therein, and not himself only but a whole kingdom, to be but a most delicate dot—he alone esteems things according to the just measure of their greatness.'

POSTSCRIPT

EGOTISM is a bastard word meant to designate something spurious and artificial, not to be confused with the natural egoism or self-assertion proper to every living creature. To condemn the latter would be to condemn life, which could not go on without it; but like every normal faculty, self-assertion has degrees, and passes insensibly from the happy mean to the opposite vices of excess and defect. Egotism, on the contrary, though more or less pronounced, is always a vice because it is founded on a mistake. It assumes, if it does not assert, that the source of one's being and power lies in oneself, that will and logic are by right omnipotent, and that nothing should control the mind or the conscience except the mind or the conscience itself. There are plausible grounds for this persuasion, to which I will return presently. It is a trap into which high speculation may easily fall, but it denies that we are created beings owing reverence to immense forces beyond ourselves, which endow us with our limited faculties and powers, govern our fortunes, and shape our very loves without our permission. Egotism is subjectivism become proud of itself and proclaiming itself absolute. There is therefore something diabolical in its courage, something satanic in its loftiness; it puffs up poor natural selfishness in the child or enterprise in the young man into a deliberate romantic madness.

That this was the moral disease which I detected in German philosophy was readily perceived in certain quarters foreign to the English-speaking world. None of my previous writings had ever been translated; but this soon appeared in French and in Italian, having attracted the attention of two Catholics, whose interest in it was chiefly, if not exclusively, religious. The ground on which I stood might be naturalistic; but they felt instinctively how much naturalism, supernaturalism, and Platonism are at one in recognizing the dependence and deceitfulness of the senses and the vain if not sinful character of worldly passions. I therefore seemed to them to be criticizing in modern terms the radical arrogance of modern philosophy, and I might prove a useful ally.

The metaphysical nature of this arrogance was wittily expressed by my French publisher. He had thought that the word *égotisme* was *rébarbatif* and might prove fatal to success with the public. The title, he said, had better be: *L'Erreur de la Philosophie allemande*, yet in order to indicate the precise error in question, he composed and put on the title-page the following motto: *Je suis, donc tu n'es pas.* This epigram subtly distinguishes egotism from brute selfishness, for no animal fighting with a rival or devouring a victim could possibly deny that his victim or rival existed. What more convincing proof that self-existence lurks in an object, than to find oneself exchanging blows with that object, or eating it and turning it into a part of one's own substance? But this collateral and equal reality between subject and object holds good in the realm of matter, where the self is the bodily person; and no idealist or solipsist would maintain that his *body* and that of his twin brother were not objects at the same level of reality and interacting parts of the same world. The degree of malice or of loving-kindness that the brothers might show would neither weaken nor strengthen the conviction of each as to the existence of the other, and the most intense selfishness in action would not lead to egotism in speculation, unless the selfish brother were a hypocrite and wished to prove that the selfishness in him was pure nobleness and holy zeal.

Egotism, then, is not piggishness or violence or any other outbreak of blind vitality, and the ego enlarged and made exclusively real by the egotist is not his physical person or self. It is a far subtler and more impersonal entity, namely the spirit to whom this whole world appears. There is a vast difference in kind and in type of reality between being a witness and being a part of the spectacle witnessed. At the theatre the audience, and even one's after-dinner self sitting there in one's evening clothes, are simply a part of the show, and perhaps the most absorbing part; yet there is always the invisible and neglected spirit that has been dragged to that place and locked up in that self and in those clothes. And the moment might come when this spirit might be aroused and might be tempted to cry —not truly, but intelligibly: *I am, therefore you are not.*

That all objects ever witnessed or loved or hated by the spirit are false objects and non-existent, has been maintained from time immemorial in India, and although in my opinion that view is wrong, or at least inacceptably expressed, there is a mystical liberation involved in it which nobody would call egotism. The ego, the self, is one of the first enemies against which a spiritual discipline must be directed, and no one could be less an egotist than the mystic who has overcome every passion and does not believe that he himself, in his separate being, has any importance or any existence.

How, then, could it come about, when the Germans, by a different approach, discovered this transcendental spirit, always well known in India, that they could fall into a pronounced egotism, psychological, moral, historical, and political? Am I perhaps hasty in saying that they rediscovered transcendental spirit at all, and did they not merely attribute transcendental prerogatives abusively to some form of the natural self?

I think that ever since Descartes uttered his *cogito*, the notion of spirit has been present in European philosophy, but undefined, sporadic, and confused with a variety of other notions. Descartes himself, in passing from *cogito* to *sum*, perhaps passed from the discrimination of pure spirit to the dogmatic assertion of his natural self, the soul or life of his body, in all its human and moral individuality. Such a transition would not be logically cogent, but it would be worthy of the naturalist and bold free reasoner that Descartes essentially was. For if there is a spirit with transcendental prerogatives, viewing and judging a world that unaccountably appears to it, surely that wakefulness and anxiety could not have broken out groundlessly in an absolute void, nor would that vision, unaccountable inwardly to the spirit, be a baseless fabric altogether. Good sense should convince us that the existence of spirit and its transcendental prerogatives express at the moral level the physical life and the physical vicissitudes of a creature bred in a pre-existing world, and feeding upon it. So that from the transcendental solitude of spirit exclaiming *I think*, Descartes could pass wisely and shrewdly, though not logically, to the assertion: *I am a thinking creature.*

In other words, this great cry, *I think*, might have been uttered by God; and that it is God and can only be God that utters it, has actually been maintained by transcendental idealism both in India and in Germany. But with what different preoccupations, and to what contrary conclusions! The Indians think that if the spirit in them is divine it behoves them to clear it of all shackles unworthy of divinity; of all partiality, of all ignorance, of all anxiety, division, or change. The Germans, on the contrary, think that if the spirit in them is divine, it lends its supreme sanction to all their desires, shares their ambitions, and ensures the fulfilment of their hopes.

Evidently that which the Indians discern and venerate is pure spirit, and if nothing compels us to follow them in their traditional ascetic and mystical discipline, calculated to bring them into perfect union or moral identity with that spirit, this happens because we have no wish for identity or union with it, but are perfectly content to be brave working and reasoning animals, as decent as possible, and to leave pure spirit alone with its loneliness. And evidently it is this homely human sentiment, with fleshly indifference to pure spirit, that inspires the Germans themselves. It always did so, and it does so now much more frankly than a hundred years ago, when their great philosophers issued their prophecies. Now official German philosophy has ceased to be theological and idealistic, without ceasing to be egotistical; for in adopting a kind of vitalistic naturalism, it has retained its trust in prophetic divination, so that the supreme destiny formerly assigned to the German race as chosen vehicles of universal spirit continues to be assigned to that race as being naturally the best, strongest, most prolific, and most artistic of races, bound therefore by natural necessity to dominate the earth.

If this prophecy were a scientific hypothesis based on positive evidence there would be nothing egotistical about it. Quite possibly one human race may be destined to survive or to enslave all the others, and I, for my part, should not be appalled if I learned on good authority that this race was to be the German, rather than the Chinese, Japanese, Jewish, or Russian. The big blond beast is an excellent beast, endowed with a first-class intelligence, sensibility, and capacity for steady work. But this is not the real ground for the German claim to supremacy. The real ground is the same that the ancient Hebrews had for proclaiming themselves the chosen people; it is clannish pride, ambition, and vanity, with the determination to encourage these passions, when in straits, by the aid of superstition. By this appeal to superstition the natural ignorant confidence that every healthy creature or nation has in itself reacts against discouragement and becomes egotism.

There are interesting symptomatic differences between the part played by superstition in German philosophy originally and the part played by it now.

In the great philosophies superstition was in the remote background, almost out of sight, because it was traditional and minimized, yet fundamental. Now it is not fundamental nor traditional nor minimized. It is introduced openly into a naturalistic *Weltanschauung* by an appeal to postulates and to myth. It is called upon to do for patriotism what, according to Bergson, *la fonction fabulatrice* does spontaneously for religion; to bolster up faint hearts and give fictitious symbolic reasons for doing that which reason could never persuade us to do. But why should any religion or national philosophy wish to deceive and mislead its adherents? If, for instance, the early Christians had been aware that they were *inventing* the speedy second coming of Christ in a cloud of glory, would they have nursed and published that illusion? Would they not have desisted at once from their attitude of expectancy, and explained that the second coming of Christ was a symbol for the spiritual life which might supervene in each man as he mortified his passions, or in the world, if it repented of its egotism? Why then over-excite and deceive the German people by *inventing* a racial myth and a providential destiny which you admit are fabulous?

An answer, heroic but perhaps not suitable for popular propaganda, might have been drawn from the philosophy of Kant, as interpreted by Vaihinger. Life, say these agnostics, must be led in the dark.

GOOD OMENS

Our senses and intellect can yield no true knowledge,
but a mysterious duty within us bids us live on nevertheless, and assume all those postulates to be true,
which, if they were true, would justify us in living.
The racial myth and the glorious prophecies now
preached to the Germans might be forms of this
categorical imperative, uttering its heroic postulates,
although secretly suspecting, if not knowing, that they
were false.

But perhaps the present is not a time for speculative
refinements. Aviators and chauffeurs have their hands
on the wheel, and in the low-lying cities and plains
there is over-population and moral anarchy. Neither
those at the top nor those at the bottom have any need
of calling upon Kant or Vaihinger for heroic motives
for living on a false faith. We must live on, we must
do something, and whatever we do will produce a
faith, false or true, in the need of doing it. When
Andromache in Homer tries to persuade Hector not
to go into the battle, because the omens are unfavourable, he replies that the best of omens is love of one's
country. And so it is, because omens, though ambiguous and casual, are signs drawn from the real world,
where events are maturing. We should never take
them for omens, if something vital and real in us did
not respond to them; and Hector would not have loved
his country as he did, unless both he and his country
had had such vitality in them as was a good omen,

though not a sure promise, of their triumph. For this reason healthy senses, normal postulates, and traditional myths, deceive us only playfully and in the most friendly and amiable way. The forms of these ideas are indeed poetical, because we are minds, and minds cannot be parts or copies of the material world that evokes them; yet the translation of facts into ideas, or of potentialities into purposes, is faithful enough, according to the proper texture of the two spheres, the one a mechanism and the other a thought.

Might not German philosophy, now so realistic in many ways, be satisfied with an honest naturalism, and cease to be egotistical? Might it not stop attributing natural performances to magic and turning history into fable? Certainly it might, if philosophy were a disembodied logic, working itself out apart from times, places, traditions, and persons. But in this case circumstances prevent. One of these circumstances, perhaps the most important, is the fact that German religion and philosophy are drawn, by a curious irony, from Jewish sources. It was the ancient Hebrews that first invented egotism, and have transmitted it to the rest of the world. Not that it appears in them at first, for egotism is a secondary thing, but they seem to have possessed from the beginning an extraordinary tenacity and fervour in sticking to life; so that although conquered, enslaved, murdered, and banished more often than any other people, they succeeded in surviving and spreading all over the world. This concentrated vitality, glowing obstinately like a spark buried deep in ashes, produced their monotheism; something quite different from the pantheism into which polytheism melts or rises in other peoples; for the one God remained their special national God; so that the creator of the world and the providence ruling over history was pledged, according to their insane persuasion, to ordain everything solely for their ultimate triumph. This is the essence of egotism, but the very enormity of such a claim, nursed in an oppressed bosom, in the midst of disasters or in solitary exile, was bound to transform itself into something more chastened and spiritual. The chosen people would end by being only the saints, even the saints of all nations, and the glory prepared for them would be a heavenly glory, essentially based on renunciation, humility, and unselfish love. Christianity could thus be grafted upon the Jewish stock, Platonism could be congruously associated with it, and something apparently contrary to all egotism could dominate religious life.

But in these matters we should not allow tone and unction to deceive us about first principles; the first principles will ultimately come to the surface. Platonism did not represent the Supreme Being as a special patron of Greece politically, yet that Supreme Being was said to be the good and the one, that is to say, the criterion of Greek morality and the principle of conceptual thinking. Was this not a national or linguistic egotism of a subtler kind? And when Christianity posited a supernatural world containing the secret powers and solving the moral problems of this life, was it not raising the interests of the human soul, and of that soul in a transitory historical phase, to supremacy over the universe? And what is this but the special egotism of repentance, taking an imaginary revenge on a too cruel world?

Thus, when the German genius at the Reformation cast off the leading-strings of Rome, and very gradually, like a good apprentice, asserted its own instincts against all borrowed traditions, it reverted from asceticism to manliness and thrift, and from supernaturalism to a conceptual philosophy of history; but up to the present time it has not discarded that original Hebraic egotism which dreamt of a chosen people and a promised land. On the contrary, it stoutly reasserts it with all the craft and patience of Jacob and all the ruthlessness of Joshua.

There is, nevertheless, a notable oscillation in the utterances of the German leaders between these cosmic claims and a frankly naturalistic view of the power and destiny of nations. All nations are conceited, and they dare proclaim their conceit on the housetops, because even the most absurd enthusiasm masters the human heart when a group of persons is at hand ready to share it. But this natural boastfulness and false courage lapse on reflection; the true interests at stake

are obviously better served by recognizing the circumstances, and therefore responsible heads will soon
limit their ambition to the possible and their self-praise
to the credible. We are all limited, we are all mortal.
Nations and individuals may have faculties that others
lack, but are sure to lack faculties possessed by others;
and the inheritance we may leave in the world—say in
religion or philosophy—is at best a seed, a self-trans-
forming force, in the later forms of which we should
never recognize our own mind. Nobody knows to
what effect the hidden forces of nature will shift the
scenes or shake the kaleidoscope. Meantime those
very forces within us prompt us to live on, and to
carry on the work which, since we were able to begin
it, we have probably the capacity to carry on and
perhaps to complete. Our character, to this extent,
is an omen of our destiny, and the more integrity we
have and keep, the simpler and nobler that destiny is
likely to be.

Such integrity, even the headstrong integrity of the
bee or the porpoise, marks a great biological triumph,
concentrating much diffuse latent vitality that matter
may contain; for in such organisms this vitality is bent
into a special vortex, endowed with stable form, and
armed with hereditary powers. This animal vitality
and this integrity can lead to egotism only when,
having become self-conscious, they arrest the spirit,
whose vocation is universal, upon their private endeavour,

and persuade it that they are supreme by their own right and initiative. The measure of harmony that in any case must exist between themselves and nature (since otherwise they would have perished), will then be attributed to their superlative merits or the special favour of heaven.

It needs no great wit to perceive what has really happened. Blind vitality in that nation has taken by chance an opportune direction and found allies in the world for a particular form of life. Such alliances are not eternal; circumstances change or vitality itself falls into a new rhythm and abandons the achieved harmony through fatigue or exhaustion, or because some fresh force has exploded within, or some accident has provoked a new experiment. When the break comes, egotism would seem to be stultified; but the Germans have always proclaimed lyrically that two souls, alas, dwell in their breast, and they have found a deep, inward justification for what, on egotistical grounds, might seem an anomaly. The absence of harmony, they say, far from proving the incidental tentative status of life in this world, is the very essence of vitality and freedom; the will, in order to will and to triumph, must perpetually struggle against itself, and posit circumstances that may defeat it. Strange that a musical nation should identify harmony with death! In fact, the German people are far from doing so in their affections, or in their homely pleasures and arts, or in their music itself; but in their hectic speculation it is very true that their spirit has always been romantic and divided against itself; now inflated, now childlike, now pedantic, and never sound in its foundations.

By this rejection of harmony as the perfection and inner principle of life, egotism passes from the metaphysical sphere, where it is a delusion of self-consciousness, to the field of politics and morals, where it represents a reversion from rational to pre-rational morality. Vitality and integrity are again to assert themselves absolutely, in defiance of their natural source and natural limits, and of the trammels that might be imposed upon them by wisdom. This is the primary tragic courage that I have described in Chapter XIV, under the name of heathenism.

Like the animal life which it expresses, pre-rational morality is far from being inwardly wicked or condemnable. On the contrary, it is the soil of all the radical virtues. There spring our primary moral judgments and admirations, our horror at this and our allegiance to that. In maintaining the wholeness and strength of a biological character once achieved, conscience and duty show their true colours. Reason cannot oppose these intuitions but may insinuate itself into them and transform them. Therefore, Socrates, the father of rational ethics, though he had clear moral and political allegiances of his own, never imposed them dogmatically upon his disciples. He begged them to speak for themselves, merely testing their consistency and pointing out the consequences. And he sought to enlighten only the Athenians, especially the very young among them, though with little success. Here, at least, he thought he knew the nature of the animal and its possible virtue, so that in appealing to spontaneous judgments he could be sure of the issue. He was never guilty of the moralistic practice of blaming fishes for liking to live under water. St Francis, when he preached to them, also avoided this error.

A romantic biologist believing in evolution (as Socrates did not) might contend that a single secret aspiration runs through the whole world and prophetically urges porpoises and flying-fish, no matter how vital and perfectly integrated their lives may already be, sometimes to break through the false roof of the sea, to draw a breath of pure air and take a peep at the sky. But I suspect that only egotistical human fancy pictures evolution in that way. In fact, some accident in growth or in the mode of chasing their prey originally led these few acrobats to take that adventurous leap, which if it proved harmless or useful, might become a hereditary practice. Yet almost all fishes, not being freaks or never having been caught in shallow or narrow waters, will continue for ever to swim contentedly under the surface, with no aspiration to turn their fins into wings or paws, to become amphibious, or eventually

like cats and flies, to develop a mortal hatred of
swimming.

Nor can the rational moralist protest against evolution
in the opposite direction, if nature should allow it.
The tadpole is more like a fish than like a frog. Might
not the frog, in a very watery marsh, develop backwards
into a fish? Our snobbish science might call it
degeneration, but in certain circumstances this physical
reversion might be a moral progress, securing greater
health, happiness, and harmony.

No doubt, reversion to any past, in the concrete, is
physically impossible, but the image of something past
or primitive may be used as a symbol, when any society
feels oppressed by alien or corrupt institutions, as
many Germans felt at the Reformation. They could
not really return to early Christianity or Judaism, yet
that illusion served to liberate something in their native
genius. So now they talk of their primitive gods and
heroes, and of a pure Aryan race; but sometimes they
admit that all this is mythical, and represents not a
fact but an aspiration. Races *become* pure, when by
selection the nobler elements in their blood are fortified
and made dominant. Apart from the dead records,
all history, no less than all policy, must be a subjective
construction, expressing like dramatic poetry some
warm intuition of the mind. Very well: impetuous
idealism thus seems to be placed in a frankly realistic
setting that, at least intellectually, is reassuring. The

moral question, however, remains open. What sort of native inspiration is it that this mythology, history, and policy come to express and to serve? Are the fables merely a political instrument in the hands of a budding theocracy, useful for keeping the popular mind entertained, and for answering verbal questions verbally, while a material aggrandisement is being secured by the secular arm? Or, beneath and beyond all this, is there a spiritual inspiration, such as the inspiration of the early Christians proved to be when, being disappointed in their material hopes of a kingdom of heaven upon earth, they understood that election or salvation was to be something moral, inherent in a change of heart, and open to all men, however childlike or wretched? In other words, is this inspiration at bottom, like that of all mature theocracies, not pre-rational but post-rational? Is it a summons to repent, to renounce the world, and to help to redeem it? The Teutonic knights are often mentioned as prototypes. What was their function, at least in theory, except to carry on in armour the same mission that the barefoot friars were carrying on in sackcloth?

Perhaps we are in the presence of something less radical than either of these alternatives and less clear in its own mind. A theocracy—and government, according to any ideology is virtually a theocracy—does not cynically invent its fables in order to deceive the people. How should the fables seem plausible unless they expressed something congruous with the popular heart? How should the prophets and priests come to conceive those fables? These men are the first to fall under that spell, transmitted from antiquity, and interwoven with all the customs and sentiments of their social world. Myths, they know, are not true in the same sense in which common information is true. Myths are intrinsically subject to expansion and transformation; every inspired prophet or preacher adds something that makes them truer and brings them nearer to what they ought to be. Their function is not to report past or future facts. Their function is rather to express the moral vicissitudes of the soul in this world, and to define, as in prayer, the demands that the soul makes by merely existing.

The demands of the soul are natural, even when they are spiritual; and even in that case the naturalist would be guilty of an egregious inconsistency if he set up his own aspirations as a duty for all other creatures. He may blazon his hereditary arms boldly and hold his own as well as may be in the struggle for life, but he must acknowledge the equal liberty of all others, at their own risk, to do the same. And if he has lived long enough in this world, he will also acknowledge the insecurity and material vanity of every achievement. Achievements, physical or spiritual, are necessarily transient. The flux of things sooner or later dissolves them; and the perfection they may have reached, seen under the form of eternity, will lose nothing for not having been universal in space, any more than perpetual in time. On the contrary, there is a sort of compensation for finitude, and an apology for instability, in knowing that numberless other opinions and ideals also must have their day.

How spirit, by its essential vocation, morally detaches itself from the self, and therefore from egotism, is clearly indicated by Schopenhauer in the radical distinction that he makes between Will and Idea. Will, in such cosmic speculations, is a metaphorical term, and stands for all physical or vital energies. Yet this Will, this psychological name for matter, plays the leading part in all German systems, and in most of those composed abroad under German influence. If, in addition, as often happens, Ideas are conceived objectively, not as living momentary perceptions but as forms of events or laws of nature or history, these idealistic systems contain no real discernment of spirit, but only an arbitrary description of nature or history in conceptual myths and psychological metaphors. Yet, in most of these philosophers the spirit is really speaking, without daring to recognize itself. It is immersed and lost in the thought of a dramatic universe, or of some particular strand within it; it takes those fatalities and that distraction for its own work, becomes in its own eyes a self-tormenting giant, and despairs of salvation. Nevertheless, salvation both from the world and from the self is close at hand, in the indomitable simplicity and actuality of the thinking spirit; and these philosophers are buoyed up and carried along by the joy of their own dark thoughts, like a poet composing a tragedy. Even in the most worldly of idealists, in Hegel, there is the universal Idea, the truth of all things, overarching that reptilian battle of concepts devouring one another which fills the nether world, and we feel that the philosopher's heart, for all his servility to the powers that be, is fixed on the truth, and clarified by that allegiance. This allegiance in Schopenhauer is more explicit, but more impatient and fantastic; for after finding freedom and joy in discriminating one Platonic Idea after another, he wilfully invites the Will to abolish itself, and to extinguish the world and the spirit together, as if blowing out a candle.

Now, soberly considered, how does this matter stand? Spirit cannot arise without being attached to some natural occasion, to give it some special aspiration and some special object; in each instance it speaks for some particular movement of life. Yet, considered in its outlook and essential vocation (which is to enlighten the Will about its opportunities and destiny), the spirit cannot hug one good only, or stand morally immovable in one place, except as it stands potentially also in other places. Thus all particular occasions and movements, with the moral perspectives open to each, are spiritually in the position that Nietzsche assigned to mankind; they are something to be superseded. Not, for the spirit, to be merely superseded historically, by another creature and another set of occasions; what could be the spiritual advantage of that? They are rather to be superseded morally, in estimation and love, by retaining only the truth about them, while escaping from egotistical immersion in their blind Will. Then all vistas together, each kept distinct from the rest, might traverse the same universe in multitudinous perceptions, crossed and incompatible if taken for forms of things, but complementary as impressions, perspectives, and signs. Diversity is normal and harmless, when the reasons for it are understood. Then all views and estimations become acceptable to the critic, as they were all generated by the facts; and he finds them convergent in their significance, both natural and spiritual, precisely because they are so various in their sensuous and moral character.

This, I believe, is the solution to egotism given by that transcendental status and function of spirit which create egotism when they are attributed to the animal Will. Not that animal Will is thereby condemned, or the vital integrity of any man or nation commanded to surrender and dissolve. But vital integrity, without being lost or emasculated, may be sweetened by charity and understanding, and the surer a man is of his soul, the more courteous he can afford to be to the souls of others. Why should we insult our fellow-creatures by asserting that their Creator abhors them and bids them become faithful copies of ourselves? Such egotistical censure would be unjust, if our rivals were true to their own genius, no matter how unpleasant their temperament might be to us, or how inconvenient their action. Our censure would become ridiculous if their action were not only true to their genius but enlightened about the circumstances and destined to lay the foundations of a new moral order. If on the contrary they, on their side, were fatuous egotists, ignorant of their destiny, our censure would be needless. Better and sooner than our wrath, their tragic impact on reality would convert or destroy them.

INDEX

A

Alexander the Great, a model for German idealists, 67
Aristotle, 103, 107
Aryan race, 167

B

Belief in God, disproved pragmatically, 116
Bergson, 158
Bull-psychology, 130–1, 135
Burckhardt, 36
Byron, 39

C

Caesar Borgia, a superman, 120
Calvinism: in Kant, 44–5; in Fichte, 14, 64; in Hegel, 96
Categorical imperative: its origin, 44; its prerogatives, 49; its dangers, 50
Chancellor, the German, his chivalrous after-thought about Belgium, 38
Christianity: foreign to Germany, 11; undermined by German philosophy, 89–90; patronized by Goethe, 34, 35; abandoned by romantic individualists, 92; denounced by Nietzsche, 113–15; has one element in common with egotism, 91
Classicism: romantic in Goethe, 35; missed by Nietzsche, 121–3; when truly vital, 36–7
Conquest, a sublime duty, 67
Contraries, alleged to be inseparable, 75
Criticism, historical, has a transcendental basis, 17–18
Critique of Pure Reason: its agnosticism, 4; its sophistical foundation, 9

D

Descartes, 155
Dürer, 16

E

Egotism: defined, x–xi; distinguished from selfishness, 80–2, 85–6, 102, 151; based on error, 149; implicit in the Kantian imperative and postulates, 49–51; implies integrity, force, self-complacency, 145–8;

INDEX

MADE AT THE
TEMPLE PRESS
LETCHWORTH
GREAT BRITAIN